New York University Studies
in Comparative Literature
III

# ❊ Ancient Greek Myths and Modern Drama

# ⁂ Ancient Greek Myths and Modern Drama

## A Study in Continuity

by Angela Belli

New York    New York University Press

London    University of London Press Limited

1969

Quotations from Eugene O'Neill's *Mourning Becomes Electra* in *Nine Plays*, copyright © 1954 by Alfred A. Knopf Incorporated. Reprinted here by permission of Alfred A. Knopf Incorporated.

Quotations from T. S. Eliot's *The Family Reunion*, copyright © 1950 by Harcourt, Brace & World, Inc. and Faber & Faber Limited. Reprinted here by permission of Harcourt, Brace & World, Inc. and Faber & Faber Limited.

Angela Belli's "Lenormand's *Asie* and Anderson's *The Wingless Victory*." Originally published in the Summer, 1967 issue of *Comparative Literature*. Reprinted here by permission; copyright © 1967 by *Comparative Literature*, University of Oregon.

Quotations from Tennessee Williams, *Orpheus Descending* with *Battle of Angels,* copyright © 1955, 1958 by Tennessee Williams. Reprinted by permission of New Directions Publishing Corporation.

Quotations from H. R. Lenormand's *Asie* in *Théâtre Complet*, Volume IX, copyright © 1938 by Editions Albin Michel. Reprinted here by permission of Editions Albin Michel.

Quotations from Jean Anouilh's *Antigone* in *Nouvelles pièces noires*, copyright © 1958 by Editions de La Table Ronde. Reprinted here by permission of Editions de La Table Ronde.

Quotations from Jean-Paul Sartre's *Huis Clos; Les Mouches,* copyright © 1947 by Editions Gallimard. Reprinted here by permission of Editions Gallimard.

Quotations from Henry de Montherlant's *Pasiphaé* in *Théâtre de Montherlant,* copyright © 1954 by Editions Gallimard. Reprinted here by permission of Editions Gallimard.

Quotations from Albert Camus' *L'Homme révolté* in *Oeuvres Complètes,* copyright © 1962 by Editions Gallimard. Reprinted here by permission of Editions Gallimard.

Acknowledgment is made to E. P. Dutton & Co., Inc. for permission to quote from *The Prodigal* by Jack Richardson. Copyright © 1960 by Jack C. Richardson. Dutton Paperback Edition. British Empire from Harold Freedman Brandt & Brandt Dramatic Department Inc.

Quotations from Maxwell Anderson's *The Wingless Victory.* Copyright 1936 by Maxwell Anderson. Copyright renewed 1964 by Gilda Anderson, Alan Anderson, Terence Anderson, Quentin Anderson, Hesper A. Levenstein. All rights reserved. Reprinted by permission of Anderson House.

To my Mother
and to the memory
of my Father

# ※ Preface

An intriguing development in the contemporary theater has been the significant use playwrights have made of Greek mythological material as the basis for new creations. The practice is hardly a new one, for in the past dramatists frequently have been attracted to the old Greek legends and have put them to various uses. But that a "neoclassical" trend should provide some of the most exciting moments in twentieth-century drama is a matter to ponder. We live in an age characterized by revolt against traditional forms and concepts and bold experimentation.

Why any artist should feel the need to cast a backward glance and resuscitate ancient material is something of a curiosity. The critic finds himself examining the artists' motives. One of the most satisfactory explanations of the peculiar appeal of myth is offered by T. S. Eliot, who resorted to the use of mythic images for his own work. Eliot's explanation comes by way of a defense of the method of James Joyce's *Ulysses*. Speaking of the use of myth to draw parallels between contemporary and ancient experience, Eliot states that "it is simply a way of controlling, of ordering, of giving a shape and a significance to the immense panorama of futility and anarchy which is contemporary history." [1] The mythical method erects "scaffolding," or skeletal structure. It is material that is organic to the work, material which can be acted upon to produce a thematic statement. In effect, myth makes art possible.

The purpose of this study is to analyze a number of plays, representative of the many written between 1900 and 1950, utilizing "the mythical method," as Eliot terms it. Varying approaches employed by playwrights adopting the method are delineated. We investigate the diverse, often intricate, convolutions — catching us unawares with new visions and new thoughts — which have been traced in the fabric of the ancient tales. We remain aware that the mythic order that underlies the new creation enables it to retain an element of the classic and reaffirm a truth which we regularly take for granted: that there is a superb continuity to our culture that is perceivable to those who can sense the presence within our age of the extraordinary achievements of the past. Link is joined to link. The matter goes beyond the recognition of so tangible a piece of evidence as, for instance, a grecian urn. It is, as John Keats saw it, a matter for the spirit.

For providing me with many invaluable insights and guidance down the labyrinthine ways of my subject, I am grateful to Thomas Bishop and Robert W. Corrigan. I wish to thank Doris Guilloton for her graciousness in reading the manuscript and offering me generous criticism and encouragement. Also I should like to acknowledge my great respect and admiration for Eric Bentley and Robert J. Clements. Through their work in comparative literature, they inspire me constantly.

[1] T. S. Eliot, *"Ulysses,* Order, and Myth," in *Forms of Modern Fiction,* ed. William Van O'Connor (Minneapolis: University of Minnesota Press, 1948), p. 123.

# ❈ Contents

# Ancient Greek Myths and Modern Drama

# ❈ I

## ❈ The Psychoanalytic Approach

Undoubtedly, one of the boldest "scandals" of twentieth-century drama is Jean Cocteau's *La Machine infernale* (1934). The author's audacity in adding to the ancient story of Oedipus a lovelorn sphinx and a ghost of the slain ruler of Thebes coupled with his ability to make these innovations dramatically significant must make us aware, despite the shock we experience from our first contact with this new version of the classical tale, that the French dramatist succeeded in writing a work of sufficient importance to our contemporary theater to invite serious attention. The play presents, aside from original conceptions in characterization and dramaturgical effects, a certain view of man which, though not a patent outlook of our time, may be the most representative, a view of man psychologically motivated, man driven by forces that he does not understand but feels compelled to obey.

In going to the Oedipus myth, Cocteau was influenced by Freudian[1] psychology, particularly the investigation of that emotional complex which Freud believed originated in a prehistoric event, the killing of the primeval father by his sons. Freud gave the discordant emotional state caused by combining unconscious drives, leading to the parricide, with

3

guilt feelings, resulting from it, the name of the Greek king, Oedipus, who, like the primeval sons committed incest and parricide. (Of course, although one may argue endlessly that the Greek hero perpetrated both acts in complete ignorance of his true parentage, supporters of the Freudian view will contend that he acted in ignorance of his own nature.) Theorists argue that the real parents of Oedipus actually resented one another and Jocasta preserved her son for the sole purpose of destroying her husband, the baby being both the object and the instrument of the couple's violent and hostile feelings toward each other.[2]

The work in the area of unconscious motivation begun by Freud was continued by others, including his one-time disciple, Otto Rank. Although Cocteau's version of the tale of Oedipus owes much to Freud, the influence of Rank's major work can be seen as all-pervasive in the French drama. In *The Trauma of Birth* (1924), Rank developed his theory that a physical trauma suffered at birth influences man's psychical life, thus providing a biological basis to Freud's theory of the unconscious. Embryonic life, according to Rank, is protective, pleasurable; birth represents an expulsion from a sort of paradise. The first contact with the cruel world at birth causes a severe shock to the helpless organism and creates an initial feeling of anxiety, named the "primal anxiety" by Rank. In some fashion, this primal anxiety erases the memory of the former blissful life of the embryo and establishes a mental barrier to the recollection of that earlier state. Whenever the powerful tendency to re-establish the intrauterine situation exerts itself, anxiety and its accompanying barrier reappear and discourage the attempt.[3] This psychical act of repression prevents us from being "unfit for life." [4] Although most people overcome the birth trauma in childhood, the neurotic does not. He yearns for the peace of prenatal life. This wish to return to the mother's womb makes itself evident in the Oedipus complex.

Anxiety, Rank continued, was turned into art in ancient Greece, for the Greeks were able, in various ways, to idealize the birth trauma. In tragedy, which takes man as its object, the repressed primal wish lives on in the milder form of tragic guilt, guilt accounting for the sufferings and punishment of the mythical hero and guilt experienced by the spectator in identification with the hero.[5] Much of Rank's thinking on this topic is disputable, of course, because he assumes that all Greeks involved in drama suffered from birth traumas. However, he is most interesting in his discussion of artistic symbols, particularly his treatment of the sphinx, which he describes as "the nuclear symbol of primal anxiety." [6] Recognized by psychoanalysis as a mother symbol, the double-formed sphinx recalls the birth anxiety.

It is useful at this point to interject a note concerning the general view of thinkers myth taken by psychoanalysis. To men like Freud, Jung, and Rank, the mythopoeic mind is psychologically motivated. Myths are regarded as collections or systems of symbols that are created in some unconscious manner and which concern human behavior. To the psychologist, myths, like dreams, are regarded as existing on two levels: "the latent" and "the manifest." The manifest content of myth is that which is discernible on the surface of the narrative; the latent content includes all symbolic undertones.

The sphinx is a symbol incorporating the essential meaning of the Oedipus myth. It is, to repeat Rank's phrase, "the nuclear symbol of primal anxiety," and it relates directly to the Oedipus complex, which Freud considered the central complex of all neuroses. It is, perhaps, the most crucial, complex, enigmatic symbol in mythology. And Jean Cocteau visualized the sphinx as a young girl in love.

The sphinx remains quite complex in *La Machine infernale*, for it is one of the three major devices of the work that serve as artistic reflections of the "primal repression" or barrier confronting the neurotic in his attempt to regress to the intrauterine garden of Eden.

The action that *La Machine infernale* celebrates, basically, is the efforts of the young Oedipe to overcome the obstacles to his regressing and becoming, despite himself, the doomed son-lover-husband of antiquity. The first act of the play, to which Cocteau gives the title "The Phantom," deals with the efforts of Laïus' ghost to contact Jocaste and Tirésias. We discover that the phantom has been materializing in defiance of supernatural commandments and with great effort for the sole purpose of warning Jocaste of the danger that is approaching Thebes in the person of young Oedipe. During those moments when it is successful in appearing, however, the ghost can be seen only by two soldiers standing guard on the ramparts of the palace; Jocaste and Tirésias are unable to see it or hear its warning. When the queen and her blind soothsayer disappear down the steps, and the spirit of Laïus disappears in forced submission to some rather mysterious, unearthly captors, never to reveal itself again, one phase of the action is completed.

The ghost is a symbol that is comprehensible on a level other than that of the literal, which does not mean simply that as a supernatural agent it has a reality beyond that of this world. In fact, as a ghost it is somewhat of a failure because it frightens no one, has a terrible time appearing and disappearing and is, if one may say so, quite frightened to death itself.

What the ghost represents, nevertheless, is central to the main action of the play and of crucial significance to the psychoanalyst's view of the complex given expression in this play reviving the myth of Oedipus. Laïus' phantom makes a desperate attempt to prevent the union of mother and son. What moves the late king to steal from his infernal resting place is precisely his inability to rest peacefully in the knowledge that his son is approaching Thebes and Jocaste. His fugitive visits to the battlements (at least five before we see him) are indicative of a spirit in great turmoil and distress. The city over which he once ruled also lies enveloped in an atmosphere of uneasiness and apprehension. People are dancing and attempting to make merry because, as the sentry tells his companion, "They can't sleep, so they dance." [7] The recent events in the city's history have created a fearful paralysis in daily activity, "this terrifying inaction" as the sentry terms it. Finally, the night-mare-ridden queen herself seems to voice a general distress, "I cannot sleep." (38).

Jocaste is restricted from joining the dancing — as Tirésias must remind her — because custom requires her to observe mourning for her dead husband, an obligation she finds difficult to fulfill: "It is too unfair" (40) is her judgment. Her resentment is such that she declares herself a victim. What she is victimized by is the necessity of acting the role of the stricken wife rather than the reveling widow she actually is. Her attitude and the essence of the act are dramatically expressed in that remarkable moment when Jocaste appears to hear the faint accents of the phantom calling out to her, "I think I hear my name." (54) However, she is too involved with the solidly physical presence of those attending her — particularly the nineteen-year-old sentry for whom she forms an immediate attachment — to heed the pleas of the rapidly fading Laïus. As she starts down towards the town and its back-street night clubs, the frustrated ghost, still shouting his vain warning, is dragged off.

All that has happened, on the literal level, is that Laïus' attempt to prevent Oedipe from marrying Jocaste has failed. However the action has a symbolic intent. The tortured, rest-less spirit of Laïus (a restlessness reflected in the life of the city) stands between Jocaste and Oedipe, barring the way to their union. As long as the spirit continues to manifest itself, creating uneasiness among the soldiers and alarming the queen, there is a possibility that it will succeed in its mission.

Furthermore, the memory of the dead king serves to check Jocaste's behavior. (Tirésias is horrified at the thought of a danc-ing queen dressed in mourning.) Nevertheless, when the moment comes for Jocaste to receive the ghost (and she has demon-strated an apparent concern for news of the apparition) she ignores it. More concerned with the young soldier and his like-ness to her son, she turns deaf ears to its cries. In ignoring the ghost, Jocaste, in effect, represses the memory of her husband, overcomes an obstacle in the path of her next marriage, and turns eagerly to the new life that awaits her. Once the spirit of Laïus is removed, moreover, balance is restored — though temporarily — in the emotional life of the city. All will accept the young king. However, that the memory of that night of Laïus' last appearance on the rampart walls lies deep within the subconscious regions of Jocaste's mind, subject to recall at the proper stimulus, is made apparent in Act III when the newly-wedded queen is heard to mumble in her troubled sleep, "This rampart wall." (126)

The unique second act, "The Meeting of Oedipus and the Sphinx," repeats the latent action of the first act. The transformed goddess of vengeance falls in love with the young mortal who reminds her of a god. Appearing in the guise of a young girl, she offers Oedipe her love. She is tired of killing and has settled on a formula for living that is apparently simple: "To love. To be loved in return by the one you love." (90) However, life is never so simple, and the unresponsive swain proceeds to complicate matters by offering his own idea of bliss: "I shall love my people; they shall love me." (90) The two views are hardly the same, as the Sphinx tries to convince the obdurate Oedipe, but to no avail. Even after she has changed into Nemesis, she is eager to accept him if he has a change of heart, but Oedipe persists in his immunity. The fact that the young man appears to be indifferent to the Sphinx does not mean, though, that she has had absolutely no effect on him. That she is a serious rival to Jocaste is illustrated in Act III when Tirésias produces the belt the young hero had left with her. In a typically uncontrollable burst of emotion, Oedipe volunteers, without being asked to, that he never promised to marry the girl. When his wife enters the room, the bridegroom guiltily hides the belt from her sight; the object makes one final appearance, in a dream that Oedipe has when he falls asleep moments later.

In addition to this image of romantic love which the Sphinx projects, a love which would prevent Oedipe from fulfilling his doom if he were to accept it, she has a latent significance. It might be useful, at this point, to recall Otto Rank's statement on the sphinx of the Oedipus legend:

> The role of the Sphinx in the Oedipus saga shows quite clearly that the hero, on the way back to the mother, has to overcome the birth anxiety, representing the barrier which the neurotic also comes up against again and again in all his attempts to regress.

> But the Sphinx, conforming to its character as strangler, represents not only in its latent content the wish to return into the mother, as the danger of being swallowed, but it also represents in its manifest form parturition itself and the struggle against it, in that the human upper body grows out of the animal-like (maternal) lower body without finally being able to free itself from it.[8]

The sphinx, then, is a mother symbol and it represents the primal trauma. Cocteau's sphinx, as we have noted, is far from being a mother symbol on the literal level; in fact, she tries to dissuade Oedipe from marrying a woman old enough to be his mother. However when the young girl mounts the pedestal and assumes the form of the sphinx, she takes on another meaning.

The Sphinx proves her power to the incredulous Oedipe by rendering him physically helpless. Although he writhes and makes frantic efforts to free himself, his paralyzed limbs will be loosened only at her consent. As Oedipe struggles fiercely before her he emulates the primal struggle of the helpless organism against expulsion from its prenatal paradise. He brings to mind that baby in Jocaste's nightmare who turns into a living paste that sticks fast to her despite all her vigorous efforts to free herself from it. Much of the Sphinx's chanting — "I unwind, I rewind. . . ." "I tie and untie and tie again. . . ." "I tighten, I let loose. . . ." "I correct, entangle, disentangle. . . ." (100–01) — take on added import when we consider her dual character of creator and destroyer. The fear of suffocation[9] must occur to Oedipe as the Sphinx explains:

"I heap up my effects until you feel that from the tip of your toes to the top of your head you are girded by all the muscles of a reptile whose slightest breath constricts yours and makes you inert like the arm on which you fall asleep." (101)

Overcome by impotence and fear, the hero instinctively calls out a name, "Mérope! . . . Mother!" (102) Yet, as soon as Oedipe feels himself free of her charm and as soon as he discovers that she has given him the answer to the riddle — and by this act she frees him — all fear and anxiety subside. A significant obstruction in Oedipe's way has been removed. Although much of the action has occurred against a background of fantasy and humor, the unmistakable mark of the play's creator, something of importance has happened to Oedipe. In his exchanges with the Sphinx, one finds a good deal more than the "witty but meaningless repartee of boulevard comedy." [10] Oedipe realizes that the swaying figure on the pedestal has lost her power over him. At that moment he loses all fear, regains his former abundant confidence, and surmounts the greatest obstacle in his path. Though he has, in effect, overcome the primal anxiety and is drawing ever closer to Jocaste, the irrational terror of his experience with the Sphinx remains at the subconscious level, and in his nightmare in the next act, he mutters the words she had chanted. Jocaste, listening to him, comments (and the irony is effective), "How he sleeps!" (163) Nevertheless, at the conclusion of Act II, the Sphinx, both as a vision of romantic love and as a dread, subliminal force, has been adequately put down.

The last impediment remaining is Tirésias. His *agon* scene with Oedipe forms a prelude to the main action of Act III. Because of the French dramatist's special use of him, the modern Tirésias — unlike his Greek predecessor — comes voluntarily to speak to an unreceptive Oedipe on the eve of his wedding. Like the spirit of Laïus, he comes to make one final and desperate plea to prevent the marriage from being consummated. The aged adviser to the queen, demonstrating here, as in the first act, a fatherly and protective attitude towards Jocaste, bases his protest on the grounds that Oedipe is not a suitable choice for the woman who is old enough to be his mother. His pointed question, "Do you love the queen?" (134) marks the beginning of an increased tension between them, culminating in Tirésias' charge, "Assassin!" and in Oedipe's violent reaction. As the surrogate father (he refers to Jocaste as "my little girl" and Oedipe calls him "grandfather") Tirésias is concerned that the queen has married a young upstart, a country lad who has, as Oedipe himself says, crashed "on Thebes like a tile from a roof!" (130) When Oedipe reveals to him what he believes to be the truth of his aristocratic parentage, Tirésias' concern for Jocaste is allayed.

Yet Tirésias is a somewhat special individual. Because he possesses both the ignorance of man and the truth of the gods, he represents a symbolic barrier that is not as easily surmounted as his human objections are. Like his Greek counterpart, Tirésias can perceive, as Francis Fergusson has pointed out, "the unrealized and therefore unrationalizable human essence beneath the masks." [11] What he can perceive are those thoughts and desires that lie suppressed and unacknowledged beneath the mask of consciousness. This is the essence of his modern magic. He can draw from Oedipe the acknowledgment that in Jocaste's love the young man feels the fulfillment of a motherly love. It is to him that Oedipe confesses the supposed truth of his background, a confession he had vowed to make to no one. Finally, in the most intensely dramatic moment of the scene, he reveals what Oedipe refuses to see — that he is intellectually and morally blind to the facts of his situation. The young man sees in the eyes of Tirésias his future only up to the point where all will be revealed. That he cannot see beyond that, despite his declared desire to read on, is due to his unwillingness to accept the reality that Tirésias brings him. When the old man begs him to reconsider his marriage, Oedipe angrily retorts: "I have her, I shall keep her, I shall find her again, and neither by prayers nor by threats can you compel me to obey orders from heaven knows where." (135)

Tirésias may well cry in despair, "Headstrong youth! You don't understand me." (133) Oedipe fails to understand that the orders he refuses to obey are from repressive forces within his psyche. Tirésias, who can penetrate the mask of consciousness to those subliminal depths where unfulfilled wishes lie, is the spokesman for that mental censor (to use Freudian terminology) by means of which the "ego" keeps the "id" in a state of unconsciousness. If Oedipe were to listen to his counsel and were able to see the light which the old man seeks to bring to him, the tragedy would be averted. However, headstrong and ambitious, under the influence of a passion he finds difficult to discuss, he denies the validity of Tirésias' arguments. One recalls the irony of his earlier statement to the Sphinx: "I must clear all obstacles, wear blinkers, and remain firm." (94) Oedipe veritably races towards tragedy.

Act II proceeds with a dramatization of the wedding night of Oedipe and Jocaste. During this scene all meanings that have remained hidden in the previous episodes come to the surface. The passion of the lovers is the incestuous love between mother and son, and the heavy sleep into which they fall is troubled with nightmarish reminiscences of their bouts with those repressive forces which sought to prevent what is actually occurring at the moment. Jocaste again has the dream of the paste that sticks fast to her, and Oedipe struggles with the Sphinx once more. That the union is an incestuous one is emphasized with repeated hints of their relationship. Jocaste's bed is covered with furs, and on the floor is an animal skin which figures in Oedipe's dreams and on which he lies face down as he watches Tirésias depart shouting his ominous warnings. Again it may be profitable to recall Otto Rank:

> Clothes made from animal material, still predominant today, prove to be a simultaneous bodily protection from the cold (which one first experienced at birth), and libidinal gratification through a partial return into the mother's warm body.[12]

In the last glimpse we have of them, we see Oedipe asleep with his head resting on the edge of the same cradle he had used as an infant, and we see Jocaste with her face against a mirror, vainly trying to make herself appear younger.

However, because Cocteau is an artist who was influenced by psychoanalytic theory rather than a psychoanalyst who wrote a play to demonstrate his thesis, *La machine infernale* does not exhibit faithfully the workings of a theory. So it is, for example, that the first barrier encountered, the Phantom, does not appear, as would be expected, to Oedipe. It seeks, instead, to be heard by Jocaste. Of course, it is true that the ghost of his father can less readily appeal to Oedipe in view of the fact that the young man never knew Laïus and would be horrified to see his ghost, let alone listen to its warning. Something else is involved however. The queen has certain impulses of her own to suppress, as we are made aware by her flirtation with the young guard who makes her think of her own son. She plays a more active part in consummating the incest than the passive Jocaste of the Greek legend, partly due to the fact that Cocteau's point of attack is an early one. His plot involves the first encounter of the doomed hero and his mother-wife. More important, the French dramatist has drawn a psychologically complex queen. Jocaste, actually, is the last obstacle standing in Oedipe's way. Sensitive to the fact of her husband's youth, she, too, could have averted the catastrophe. The last sound we hear at the end of Act III is a drunken voice singing a warning to the bride: "Your husband's too young/Much too young for you." (166)

However Jocaste welcomes the match. She ignores the same warnings as those received by Oedipe and demonstrates the same compulsion to satisfy subconscious drives. By exhibiting two strong willed individuals moving toward each other and ignoring all checks on their progress, Cocteau creates drama. He also creates tragedy, for tragedy results when all barriers have been shattered and Jocaste and Oedipe have both realized their desire. Interestingly enough, the only comment on their act, a comment which indirectly pleads for acceptance without censure, comes from the ghostly queen at the conclusion of Act IV: "Things which appear abominable to human beings, if only you knew, from the place where I live, if only you knew how unimportant they are." (188)

Mother and son, through all the confrontations of the preceding acts, have been moving towards the moment which
occurs in Act IV, the unmasking of Oedipe as murderer and
son. Events are telescoped. Oedipe's realization of his situation
is immediate; its immediacy is believable, also, because he has
been presented as dimly aware throughout the previous acts,
as has been Jocaste, of his inner turmoil. All fears have remained just below the level of consciousness, and in this last
act, Oedipe is able to recall Jocaste's "linen-maid" story of so
many years before; he also recalls his encounter with Tirésias
on the eve of his wedding and tells him, "I see it all clearly
now, Tirésias." (186)

The play is so structured that dramatic unity results from
a repetition of the same symbolic action in the first three acts
and a resolution of that action in the final act. In Acts I, II, and
III, the individual is confronted with a force that seeks to
inhibit his impulses and prevent the tragic action from being
accomplished. The symbols used — the Phantom, the Sphinx,
Tirésias — have a double value; yet, in both their manifest and
latent meanings, they retain their identity as impediments.
The individual successfully surmounts both the evident obstacle, that is, that obstacle which is apparent on the literal
level, and the deeper, subliminal restriction, which is a reflection of that original represser, the primal anxiety. The aim of
the three double-sided figures created by Cocteau is the same
as that of the initial force identified by Rank, namely, the
prevention of the incest. However the incest occurs anyway.

Faced with the facts, Oedipe and Jocaste destroy themselves
in the same way as do the Greek characters. However, another note is introduced by Cocteau in the final moments of his
drama. The Voice opens the act with the pronouncement that
before the curtain comes down we are to witness the transformation of the player-card king into a man. "Man" and his
development from infancy to old age is the answer to the
Sphinx's riddle, but the young Oedipe, paralyzed and fearful
before the terror of the Sphinx, cannot reply to her celebrated
question. Unlike the classical hero who uses his intelligence to

arrive at the solution, Cocteau's Oedipe has to be told the answer, and the answer to the Sphinx's riddle answers the riddle of *La machine infernale*. Otto Rank maintains that individuality and autonomous will develop as the child grows away, physically and psychologically, from the mother.[13] Oedipe is able to become a man, finally, and answer for himself the riddle of his own existence through a realization of the truth and an abrupt and decisive separation from Jocaste. He attains in the last act of the drama an insight that he lacked in the Sphinx scene. After hearing the Shepherd, he quickly pieces together, by himself, the answer he has been seeking: "I have killed whom I should not. I have married whom I should not. I have perpetuated what I should not." (183) He has fulfilled the Voice's prophecy.

The last act, which follows so closely the action of Sophocles' *Oedipus Rex*, serves to underline a fundamental difference between Cocteau's play and the Greek tragedy in that what has formed the primary movement for the pattern of action of the Greek work, that is the finding of Laïus' slayer,[14] now becomes a secondary theme. In the French drama, Cocteau has the slain Laïus himself appear at the beginning of Act I and speak, however briefly and disconnectedly, about the young man in question. What the spectator views is not the gradual discovery of the hero's error but the progressive creation of that error. All action moves towards that moment in the last act when the main character discovers that his inability to comprehend his true nature has caused him to make the wrong decisions. Cocteau's hero is destroyed because he submits to his unconscious drives, which propel him across his father's path and into his mother's arms. He is a victim of that form of psychic determinism that stresses unconscious motivation. In addition to the scientific explanation of Oedipe's downfall, Cocteau offers another. As the title of the play suggests, Oedipe and Jocaste are victims of a malignant fate, an enigmatic force that manifests itself long enough to strike at helpless man. Persecuted by the gods, at the mercy of obscure internal drives, man's destruction is inevitable.

Cocteau emphasizes the certain working out of fate by informing the spectator in advance of what is going to happen and by allowing the forecasted events to unfold inevitably as the drama progresses. The chorus-like Voice relates the entire tale before the action begins. In the second act, it is the mysterious god Anubis — another contribution of Cocteau's to the myth which is striking in its originality — who tells an eager Sphinx of the past and future of Oedipe and Jocaste. Less specific, several hints of impending gloom are given throughout the play. Foreshadowing is accomplished during such moments when Jocaste encounters the young guard and dreams of her son and when Oedipe begins to read his future in Tirésias' blind eyes. The purpose of informing the spectator in advance of the action to follow serves to minimize suspense and uncertainty as to the ending reserved for the hero and allows for a more concentrated attention to each of his encounters with the forces and characters which are to contribute to that ending.

If there is any external, human force that could possibly influence the behavior of Cocteau's characters, it is the society in which they must function. The representatives of that society are the two sentries, ordinary citizens of Thebes who possess the power, for one brief moment, to enlighten their queen and thwart whatever destiny hovers over the scene. As Act I closes — the Phantom has been dragged off; Jocaste has gone dancing; and we are a giant step closer to the catastrophe — one of the soldiers proposes to his companion that they repeat the Phantom's message, word for word, to Jocaste, who did not hear it. The older man replies, "Let princes deal with princes, phantoms with phantoms, and soldiers with soldiers." (64) Tragedy is indeed unavoidable when man lacks the ability to relate to his fellow man.

Considerations about the sentries call to mind an example of Cocteau's method of bringing his mythological material close to ordinary reality. The soldiers who stand guard at the Theban palace speak a modern, colloquial prose. Their frequent use of slang gives them a familiar aspect: they resemble soldiers whom the spectator has met in his own time. A num-

ber of anachronisms are scattered throughout the work. The
sentries, and later Jocaste herself, listen enviously to the sound
of music coming from the popular night clubs of the city,
where the citizens of Thebes amuse themselves. The Matron,
who has a brief encounter with the Sphinx, complains to her
about the economic depression which has gripped the city.
The woman may be talking about the difficulty of living in
Thebes during the time of the Sphinx's terror, but somehow her
remarks about rising costs, the lack of government control, and
the failure of business enterprises, among other things, have a
modern, twentieth-century ring. Suddenly the myth loses some
of its remoteness.

One element, a very strong one, separates *La Machine
infernale* from the ancient legend and helps create the impression that the French Oedipus is to be regarded with something
less than seriousness. Except for the last act, where the tone is
predominantly somber and austere, the preceding acts have
been played out in an atmosphere of fantasy, mystery, and
humor, an atmosphere which veils the complexity of the myth.
The young Oedipe and his frivolous queen are figures taken
from Greek mythology but repainted in bold, glaring colors.
Their respective encounters with the Sphinx and the Phantom
are played out in a semifarcical tone. Critic Jean Borsch la-
ments the fact that the supernatural and the intervention of
gods and fate is treated with considerable "levity." [15] However
it is precisely through the humor and the levity that Cocteau
heightens the tragedy. Irony is created when one contrasts the
apparent lightness of many of the scenes with the starkness of
fate.

The author's ingenuity in creating a unique style is, by
now, a legend unto itself, yet the spectator who allows himself
to become dazzled by the spectacle is apt to receive several
jolts during the course of a performance of *La Machine infernale*. Take, for example, the first act. The initial observation
to be made is that Cocteau, tongue in cheek, glint in eye, is
parodying the first act of *Hamlet*. Resisting the temptation to
make that inevitable connection between the hero of the play

the French writer is parodying and the hero of his own drama, we pass on to the sparkling dialogue of the sentries. The humor here is particularly broad, especially when the men demonstrate their affection for the ghost and their inability to facilitate his disappearance by cursing at him (because cursing is a tender mode of expression among soldiers). However, one need only recall that the city the guards look down upon is ancient Thebes and the ghost whose visits they eagerly await is the spectre of the cursed Laïus to be involved suddenly and fixedly within the reality of the myth. Tirésias may be a tottering old man obliging the wishes of a petulant Jocaste, but his significance becomes striking in the third act when, chafing at the young Oedipe who seeks to exert his temporal authority, the sooth-sayer announces, following the example of his Greek counter-part, that he serves only the gods.

George Steiner would seem to be missing the point when, referring indirectly to Cocteau, he condemns contemporary playwrights for having ". . . ancient myths appear in the mod-ern playhouse either as a travesty or an antiquarian charade." [16] What is actually the case in La Machine infernale is that the "travesty" and the "charade" surround the myth, obscure it so to speak, in order that its essential meaning, as Cocteau appre-hends it, can be perceived on a higher level. The author is working with the poetic device of symbolism, and because symbolism involves the presentation of one idea by means of another, the thoughts we entertain may be somewhat distant from the immediate experience of the work. There is a danger, of course, in that kind of criticism which perceives symbols everywhere and attributes unconscious motives to characters (and sometimes to authors as well); the critic may succeed in producing a creation rather than an interpretation and end by pleading unconsciousness himself. However, when the discrim-inating spectator finds himself confronted with a decidedly Freudian Oedipus, it behooves him to remain lucid and keep an open mind to the possibility that the author deliberately pre-sented his character from a psychoanalyst's point of view and, in so doing, incidentally alchemized science into art, travesty being his secret ingredient.

The Oedipus myth was not the sole one to seize the attention of psychoanalysts. Theorists found in the ancient tale of the doomed house of Atreus matter for observation. What appeared to be evidence of neurotic behavior was discerned in the affection of Atreus' granddaughter, the princess Electra, for her father, Agamemnon, and in her hatred of her mother, Clytemnestra. The psychic disorder which, in a girl, corresponds to the Oedipus complex became known as the Electra complex. Like Cocteau, the American dramatist, Eugene O'Neill, was struck by the possibilities for art present in the psychoanalytic observation of a myth. Accordingly, in *Mourning Becomes Electra* (1931) he exposed to view the history of a powerful American family, the Mannons, created as a parallel to the Greek family of Atreus. Infusing his work with that same sense of impending doom that Cocteau managed so successfully and that is inherent in earlier versions of the story (particularly that of Aeschylus) O'Neill demonstrated the pernicious effects of subliminal drives.

The first challenge facing O'Neill was the creation of an event in the family's past history capable of producing the same violent future repercussions as those initiated by the offenses within Atreus' family (Thyestes' seduction of Atreus' wife; Atreus' retaliatory action against his brother, the slaughter of his two children; and the ensuing murders). The civilized barbarism O'Neill devised (civilized because it occurs in New England) was the treatment by Abe Mannon of his brother, David, who had won the love of the Canuck nurse, Marie, whom Abe desired for himself. The unsuccessful lover turned his brother and Marie out of the family, tore down the house in which their love had been born, and cheated David out of his inheritance. David's response was to hang himself. This action, anterior to the play's opening, creates a pattern of psychological motivation, frustrated wishes, and mental torture out of which O'Neill fashioned an American parallel to the Greek tale.

Much of the power of O'Neill's work results from his ability to create the same atmosphere of foreboding and impending gloom that permeates the ancient legend. *Mourning Becomes Electra* opens with the watchman of the Mannons, Seth, conducting some town cronies on a forbidden tour of the estate. He has already received the news that the war, the Civil War in this case, has ended and he wants to celebrate the return of the head of the Mannon household, a Yankee general. When Ezra Mannon's daughter, Lavinia, tells the old servant that it is indeed time that her father come home, Seth answers with a keen glance and a slow "ayeh," and we hear a familiar note of foreboding. The theme of the classical story which the American dramatist seized for his own purposes is that of the past as an all-present reality and as a menace to the future of Agamemnon's family. O'Neill makes use of a number of devices to demonstrate the intrusion of the past upon the present. He begins by making use of Seth; the watchman has Lavinia recall the old scandal about David and Marie. Then he reveals that Adam Brant, the Aegisthus of the American drama, is the product of the ill-fated couple's marriage. Because the dashing Captain Brant, a remnant of the Mannon past, is very much involved in the present life of Christine Mannon, O'Neill's Clytemnestra, Seth's information introduces the first concrete bit of ominous news.

The major device the playwright uses to show the past at work in the present is the "repetition of the same scene — in its essential spirit, sometimes even in its exact words, but between different characters — following plays as development of fate. . . ." [17] O'Neill uses repetition in a different way than Cocteau to achieve the same end. In *La Machine infernale,* it is the symbolic action, that is the character unknowingly confronting repressive forces, which is repeated, and the author, aside from telling us that the first two acts occur at the same time, makes no mention of the fact that it is the same action that is taking place. However, in *Mourning Becomes Electra,* it is that surface action that is repeated because action occurs on only one level; one is constantly aware of this repetitive movement, even if the author had not made his purpose clear in his notes. The characters themselves speak of what is happening, as Doris M. Alexander has noted.[18] Because O'Neill constructed a trilogy, repetition occurs from play to play, and by repeating in a later play or scene a phrase or an action from an earlier one, the dramatist is able to achieve a sense of perspective throughout the three plays. Beginning initially with the past, which exists before the play opens, he develops an atmosphere of gloom and foreboding which forms the background for the present, which unfolds in *Homecoming*. That present subsequently becomes the past of *The Hunted* and of the final play, *The Haunted*, such as the moment when Lavinia tells Orin, in Act I, Scene ii of the third play that they must forget the past and make an effort to begin a new life. What she is doing is repeating Ezra's futile plea to his wife on the eve of his homecoming.

The purpose of creating patterns of repetition is to show the family progressing, generation by generation, towards its doom. The Mannons resemble each other in that they have the same unconscious drives; they impose on their compulsions the same code of society-approved restrictions, the code of Puritanism, which clashes with their temperament. Another way in which O'Neill creates a living past is by having his characters bear a striking physical resemblance to one another and to their ancestors. Orin, Brant, and Ezra possess common physical characteristics that can also be detected in the faces of the Mannon ancestors whose portraits hang on the walls of the sitting room. And the Mannon women, Christine and Lavinia, possess the same beautiful hair and eyes that made Marie so attractive to Abe and David Mannon. Doris M. Alexander raises the question that comes to the spectator's mind as he notes the physical and even the psychical resemblance between the members of the different generations, namely, why it is inevitable that Ezra and Adam both love Christine, and that Christine and Lavinia both love Adam. She suggests that the answer may lie in *What Is Wrong with Marriage* by G. V.

Hamilton and Kenneth Macgowan, where one finds the notion that a man's mother and a woman's father determine the type of mates each will choose. Thus Ezra loves Christine because she resembles Marie Brantôme, a mother image. Adam resembles Ezra; therefore, Lavinia loves Adam.[19] The critic's conclusion that O'Neill, through a repetition of patterns, conveys to the audience the idea that his characters are psychologically trapped is sound, although one may question the reasoning that leads to the conclusion.

Because we are going to consider Marie Brantôme in any discussion of the current Mannons — and it is imperative that we do — we must go over the references to the old scandal. If the Canuck nurse served as a mother image for young Ezra, was she similarly important to Abe and David? The tragic chain of events is initiated by the rivalry between the two brothers for the same girl. Following the logic of *What Is Wrong with Marriage,* one must conclude that both men loved Marie because she reminded them of their mother. Nothing of the sort is suggested. Actually, we do know enough about the Mannon temperament, beginning with that of Abe's, to determine how the fatal attraction for Marie and the women who resemble her came about.

Doris Falk has explained, quite appropriately, that the Mannons are trapped by the tension of such opposites as the conscious and the unconscious mind.[20] Let us attempt, therefore, to discover what the unconscious mind of the Mannons is like, an unconsciousness which lies hidden beneath the mask-like expressions their faces assume. A clue is provided in the fact that they are a family of ship builders. Abe Mannon built up the family fortune in shipping, starting one of the first Western Ocean packet lines, as Seth relates. The influence of the sea, frequently a theme in other O'Neill plays, has shaped the Mannon character, and the sea functions symbolically in this play as a means of "escape and release."[21] Basically, the men are romanticists who respond to the call of the exotic. The vision of paradise that they each carry is that of the South Sea Islands. Adam Brant is the captain of a clipper ship, and

Lavinia describes him to Peter in the following manner: "He went to sea when he was young and was in California for the Gold Rush. He's sailed all over the world — he lived on a South Sea Island once. . . ." [22] When Peter remarks that "he seems to have had plenty of romantic experience," Lavinia retorts: "That's his trade — being romantic!" (697) Brant, who dresses "with an almost foppish extravagance, with touches of studied carelessness, as if a romantic Byronic appearance were the ideal in mind," (703) frequently confuses women and ships. He speaks dreamily of "tall, white clippers" that remind him of "beautiful, pale women." And he tells Lavinia: "Women are jealous of ships. They always suspect the sea. They know they're three of a kind when it comes to a man!" (705)

What Brant finds appealing in the Mannon women is a physical trait they share with his mother, "big, deep, sad eyes that were blue as the Caribbean Sea!" (704) Abe Mannon fell in love with Marie's exoticism also. Her French and Canadian background and her character appealed to him. Seth describes her as being "frisky and full of life — with something free and wild about her like an animile." (728) Christine shares not only physical traits with Marie, but also her free and wild nature. The women the Mannons marry stand in sharp contrast to the local New England girls represented by Louisa, the wife of one of the town cronies, who voices the opinion of the community when, commenting upon Christine's French and Dutch ancestry, she proclaims that Ezra's wife is "furrin lookin' and queer." (690) Another example of the local variety is provided in the unflattering portrait of the wife of Josiah Borden, who is described as "a typical New England woman of pure English ancestry, with a horse face, buck teeth and big feet, her manner defensively sharp and assertive." (753) Ezra, too, had once responded to the call of the exotic, and Christine, before her marriage, found him "silent and mysterious and romantic!" (714) There is a two-way attraction between the romantic Mannons and the women they choose.

When Lavinia finally realizes the Mannon dream, in *The Haunted*, and goes to the South Seas, she meets one of the ship's officers on the voyage. His name is Wilkins, and at the sight of him Lavinia discards her mourning and buys new clothing that flatters her. Orin knows her motive. Wilkins reminds her of Brant, he charges: "Adam Brant was a ship's officer, too, wasn't he? Wilkins reminded you of Brant. . . ." (714) Lavinia denies that she was attracted to Wilkins, but we know that she is lying. What is interesting, however, is that no word is mentioned of a physical or even a spiritual resemblance between Wilkins and Brant (not to mention Wilkins and Ezra). The only point of similarity that Orin mentions is the fact that both men are sailors.

Finally, the Mannon house, built by Ezra in fury and hatred, is in the Greek Revival style, a lovely mode that became popular in early America when this country's sympathies for Greece, fighting for her life against the Turks, were stirred by Byron's poems on her plight, and feelings became so frenzied that towns throughout the young republic began taking Attic names like Athens, Euclid, Sparta, and Troy.

What creates the frustrations and complexes of the play is the suppression and denial of the romantic impulse and the acceptance of the narrow Puritan view of life, a distorted Puritanism that is subscribed to only as a means of rationalizing uglier feelings. When Lavinia calls her murder of Brant an act of justice, she merely resorts to that same defense mechanism her grandfather had used years before when he cast his brother and Marie out of the house. Abe acted as a proud, jealous, vengeful individual, but as a sanction for his act he invoked the Puritan code of the community. As the town's leading citizen, he had to continue upholding its standards; so every Sabbath he took his family to the white meetinghouse to meditate on death. The young Ezra was made to learn the Puritan creed that "life was a dying. Being born was starting to die. Death was being born." (738) No wonder he was a poor lover! He, too, had been involved in the family's shipping business, but when he returned from the Mexican War to discover that love no longer existed in his marriage, he turned to other occupations; he became judge and mayor of his Puritan town, and once more a Mannon reluctantly became an upholder of the community code.

The gloomy atmosphere in which Ezra had been raised so warped his emotions that he confused love with lust, ruined his marriage, and created an environment of hatred and deception in which his children, born to a mother who loathed her husband, were raised. Christine's transference of her love from her husband to her son and Ezra's similar act of displacement — or sublimation — of love from his wife to his daughter is responsible for the Oedipus and Electra complexes from which Orin and Lavinia suffer. The destructive illusion that misleads the Mannons is the sham Puritan existence they lead; the reality they deny is their romantic natures.

That the Mannons are frustrated in love is undeniable. The nature of their inevitable doom, though, is rather complex, involving another factor. If unrequited love were sufficient to cause the family's tragedy, the opposite, success in love, should create great joy. However when Adam Brant comes to realize that running off with Christine means giving up his ship, he feels quite dejected. As he embraces her, after they have made their decision to flee, Adam is seen to stare over her head "with sad blank eyes." (799) Also, the only successful lover in the family, David Mannon, who had the fortune to win the charming Marie, expressed his bliss by hanging himself. Obviously love is not enough. What caused David to despair was the fact that he had been cut off — both financially and spiritually — from his family and, ultimately, from the surrounding society. Abe's jealousy and the prudishness of the close-minded community made him feel alone; unable to take increased strength from his wife and son, he turned on them.

Adam describes his father's fall: "He'd taken to drink. He was a coward — like all Mannons — once he felt the world looked down on him. He skulked and avoided people." (708) Brant goes on to describe an incident when David, particularly drunk one evening, turned and struck his wife. His son promptly picked up a poker and landed a blow on his head. Later, a remorseful David asked Adam to forgive him, but his son refused. Soon afterwards, they found David hanging in the barn. The last blow for him was that administered by his son. Feeling himself completely deserted and unable to exist in a world in which he played no vital role, he took his life. Nevertheless, the blame for David's tragedy — his own weakness apart — must go to the brother who first denied him his fortune and place within the family. Further, by refusing to accept his brother's marriage, Abe set an example for the community to follow in condemning David's morals. The original offense in the Mannon family and that which initiates the chain of unhappy circumstances is a crime against family ties — as it is in the Greek legend.

The Mannons' doom, and O'Neill is quite specific about it, is "the separateness, the fated isolation of this family." [23] Frustration in love alone could not create such isolation, for it never does. Many people who are unhappy in love have the capacity to rechannel their strong feelings in other directions. The Mannons have that capacity, as pointed out previously. Of course, unhappiness in love does create a general unhappiness, but O'Neill does not concern himself primarily with such despair, nor does he make it the ultimate doom of the family, which otherwise parallels that of Atreus. What most interested the American playwright was a study of the inevitable destruction of a once proud family, a once powerful family. In an attempt to explain that inevitability he had to devise what he considered to be a modern concept of fate, acceptable in the light of modern theories of human behavior. What we can say regarding the characters' frustrations is that their unstable emotional lives separate them from society and from one another, and it is this separateness that is their ultimate tragedy, a separateness toward which they are propelled by their own temperament.

Significantly, O'Neill altered the myth so that his Orestes does not face the same dilemma that caused the Greek character so much torment. The awful dilemma in which the classical hero finds himself is that he must and yet he must not murder his mother. O'Neill's Orin faces no such dilemma. He does not feel duty bound to avenge the father he never loved, and far from killing his mother, he unwillingly drives her to suicide. Orin murders the Aegisthus of the American drama not to avenge his father's murder but to avenge himself; Brant has robbed him of his mother's love and he acts, like his grandfather before him, out of pure hatred and jealousy. Similarly, in goading him on, Lavinia seeks a retaliation for the loss of her father's love and revenge for Brant's treachery to her and his lack of response to her love for him.[24]

The death of Christine occurs after that of her lover, and the fact that she is a suicide highlights the difference between the Greek legend and the American drama. Christine is much weaker than the strong-willed Greek queen; her death results not from the workings of a law which imposed on the son a grievous duty to avenge his father's murder, but from her realization that no happiness is possible for her in a world where her lover is dead and those responsible for his death are a son who is mentally unbalanced and who desires her love selfishly and exclusively, and a daughter who loathes her. If she is to continue living, Christine must suppress completely and finally that romantic impulse which was to have carried her off with Brant to the South Seas via the ship "Atlantis." She must accept the Mannon lot — complete alienation from all that her nature propels her towards. Her inability to do so drives her to suicide.

There is much that is sympathetic about Christine. O'Neill has seized on one of the motives that drove the Greek heroine to commit crime, that is, love for Aegisthus. However, he has softened the moral condemnation that descends upon his Clytemnestra for the betrayal of her husband by demonstrating that a marriage in which both partners are temperamentally incompatible is doomed to be dissolved, whether that dissolution occurs according to legal means or not, and by dramatically illustrating the destructive effects of such a union, not only upon the husband and wife but upon the children as well.

Similarly, Adam Brant is sympathetically presented. Although his original motive in winning Christine was to avenge Ezra's treatment of his mother, he comes to feel a genuine love for her. O'Neill says of his Aegisthus that Adam is "more human and less evil" [25] than his Greek counterpart. Indeed he is, for he has none of the Greek usurper's political ambition. The only motive regarding material gain that could be attributed to him — the cheated patrimony — is justifiable and is, in fact, regarded as a just motive in the ancient legend where it is attributed to Orestes himself. This transference of motive from Orestes to Aegisthus is an attempt on O'Neill's part to strengthen Brant's character and make him more palatable; it also serves to keep the family's past transgressions before our eyes at significant moments, such as that when Brant's reserve breaks down and he bitterly denounces Abe Mannon to Lavinia.

Sympathetic as Christine and Brant are at the outset, however, they do murder Ezra, and it is Christine's decision to murder her husband that condemns her. Brant is a reluctant accomplice, though an accomplice nevertheless. Christine decides that she must be free of Ezra, and even his avowal that he has changed his ways has no effect upon her decision. It is an irony that Ezra, quite as morally blind as Agamemnon, does not discover until it is too late how he can save his marriage. He appears to be guilty of few of the grave offenses for which the Greek king is punished. He does not tread on purple carpets, butcher his children, or return with a captive southern girl as the spoils of victory. However, we cannot regard his other faults lightly, and close scrutiny reveals a nature not fundamentally unlike that of the Greek king. General Mannon's fierce and false pride, coupled with his narrow-mindedness and slavish adherence to the death-in-life philosophy of his father, makes him as deserving of his wife's hatred as Clytemnestra's husband. We can believe Christine when she states that Ezra, out of pure spite would never agree to give her a divorce.

Aside from inspiring his wife with contempt and disgust

for him, Ezra attempts to loosen the ties between his son and Christine by trying to make something of a man out of the weak Orin. He has him join the army. A certain similarity may be detected between Christine's feelings regarding the loss of her son's love and Clytemnestra's fury at the brutal slaughter of Iphigenia, but the parallel is a slight one. There is no doubt that Christine resents Ezra's interference, but Orin's loss is in no way comparable to the loss of Iphigenia who, unlike Orin, dies a sound death, nor does his mother react to his absence as did the grieving queen to the loss of her daughter. Orin may be temporarily away from the Mannon house, but he is never lost to Christine and she knows it. Although she may have missed him at first, Orin's absence merely provides her with an additional excuse for hating her husband. As soon as Orin is home, his first thoughts are to assure her of his love (even before he can bring himself to view his father's body). She responds by encouraging his attentions toward Hazel. Orin then accuses his mother of trying to free herself of him: "'I'm not home an hour before you're trying to marry me off. You must be damned anxious to get rid of me again!" (771) When Christine protests that she has been terribly lonely without him, he adds that she has written only two letters to him within the past six months. Regardless of any resentment Orin feels for his mother, whatever the grievance, Christine always manages to soothe him. It is not long before he confesses that he equates the South Sea island of his dreams with Christine herself. He tells her: "The breaking of the waves was your voice. The sky was the same color as your eyes. The warm sand was like your skin. The whole island was you." (776) The passage may be remembered as an example of O'Neill's unsuccessful attempts at lyricism, but it is also the clearest statement of Orin's abnormal attachment to his mother, and through the use of a recurrent symbol it calls to mind the basic conflict of the Mannons. O'Neill has captured the soul, if not the letter, of poetry.

What Orin desires most is to resume that relationship with his mother that he enjoyed as a child. Christine and her son had withdrawn into a secret world of their own, in voluntary isolation from the rest of society. Orin gleefully recalls their private rule: "No Mannon allowed was our password, remember!" (772) Unconsciously, he shared the neurotic's wish for that prenatal peace and security that the South Sea island symbol also represents. (The symbol is a complicated one because it embodies different ideals for different Mannons.[26] For Orin it signifies that paradise where he can achieve an exclusive and permanent maternal love.)

When Orin finally does make the actual voyage to the islands with Lavinia, after his mother's death, he finds none of the serenity he had anticipated. Without his mother, he could not find the joy he had found in his dreams. The pale and haggard Orin describes his experience upon his return: "We stopped a month. But they turned out to be Vinnie's islands, not mine. They only made me sick — and the naked women disgusted me. I guess I'm too much of a Mannon after all, to turn into a pagan." (831) We cannot for a moment believe that Orin has turned into a Puritan. What he means is that without his mother he has become separated from the one individual with whom he found happiness. He, too, has become a Mannon circle of insularity, and he shares the family doom.

The fits of madness, which increased during his voyage, cause Orin to have a complete collapse. The Furies that torment him are pangs of conscience for the death of Christine. Even though Christine commits suicide willingly and gladly, Orin feels as much responsible for her death as the Greek prince who slaughtered his mother with an axe. Unlike his classical counterpart, his madness is in no way brought on by memories of the horror of his father's death but by his mother's suicide and his realization that his dream of paradise on earth is lost to him. He resolves on seeking his vision further, and he kills himself.

Much of the dramatic intensity of *The Haunted* derives from the character transformation apparent in Lavinia and Orin. Lavinia loses her stiff Puritan manner and comes to bear a striking resemblance to her mother; similarly, Orin now resembles the father he hated so. The psychological device at

work is that of introjection, whereby an individual identifies
himself with someone else. In Orin's case, the identification
has come about because of his realization of a fundamental
kinship with his father. As the counterpart to Oedipus, he
rivals his father for his mother's love. The visual identification
is completed when he experiences that terrible loneliness which
was Ezra's fate. Lavinia imitates her mother consciously because she had always felt an unconscious kinship with her.
Christine is outwardly the romantic, spontaneous creature that
lies latent within each Mannon. And it is because of that
romantic impulse within Lavinia that Captain Brant was attractive to her. With Lavinia, the transformation is completed
during the trip to the islands, which Brant loved, when she
responds to "the warm earth in the moonlight . . . the surf on
the reef . . . the natives dancing innocent — without knowledge of sin!" (834)

Oscar Cargill finds Lavinia's transformation incredible. He
questions whether it is possible for a woman possessed of a
New England conscience to slough off the sense of guilt for the
murder of Brant and the suicide of her mother and joyfully turn
to an acceptance of life. The Electra of Euripides merely
touches her brother's sword and she realizes that she cannot
hope for any happiness thereafter. Cargill questions, What are
the Erinyes compared to a New England conscience? [27] O'Neill
is doubtless to blame for such puzzlement. Lavinia's transformation is abrupt and clumsily handled (as is Orin's), for the
American playwright's use of the psychological mechanism is
somewhat immature. However the implication of the scene is
that if Lavinia appears joyful, unnaturally so considering her
past crimes, it is because she is no longer Lavinia, but Christine. So completely has she assumed her mother's character
that remorse — that same emotion which was alien to Christine
following Ezra's murder — is now alien to her also. Nevertheless
the Erinyes that are to assail her will exact their due punishment. When Lavinia comes to realize that love is never sinful
she discards the mask of the Puritan and confronts her true self.
The view is a fleeting one, though, for O'Neill will not allow

his Electra to "peter out into undramatic married banality." [28]
Criticizing that development in the Euripidean version of the
myth where Electra marries Pylades, the American dramatist
questions why the Furies should have allowed Electra to escape
unpunished.

Dwelling on the problem of extending retribution beyond
the limits traditionally set by the Greek versions of the tale,
O'Neill turned once more to implementing his device of repetition. As Lavinia and Peter are embracing, after having declared their love for each other, Orin bursts unexpectedly into
the room. Half choking with jealous rage, he manages to control himself with some effort. The scene is a repetition, with
different characters in different roles, of a moment that occurs
towards the end of *Homecoming*. There Lavinia had surprised
her mother and father in a similar embrace. Managing to dis-
guise her jealous hatred before her father, she cries out her
loathing and disgust once she is alone. She resolves that it is
her duty to inform Ezra of her mother's affair with Adam.
Motivated by the same fierce jealousy, Orin first offers his surprised sister and Peter his felicitations, but it is not long before
he is hard at work on his detailed report of the Mannon history,
which is to include details of all of Lavinia's transgressions.
He intends to show the document to his sister's beau and thus
prevent the wedding from taking place. It is the past which is
deciding Lavinia's future, however she may attempt to escape it.

Having lost Christine, Orin transfers his abnormal love
from his mother to his sister. Conditioned from childhood to
respond to Christine's charms, he responds to the stimulus
created when Lavinia appears to reincarnate the dead woman.
Such action is completely foreign to the Greek myth. Oscar
Cargill reminds us that the incest theme was first treated by
Robinson Jeffers in *The Tower Beyond Tragedy* (1925).[29] In
*Mourning Becomes Electra* we appreciate another use of the
dramatic potential inherent in incest. Lavinia reacts to Orin's
incestuous love with disgust. That disgust is tinged with a new
element that first appears here. She is horrified at the spectacle

of her brother's madness and the growing realization that the torture he is suffering is a prelude to her own.

Lavinia is by far the most forceful character in the play. She, rather than Orin, performs the most important action of the plot. O'Neill's character resembles the Greek heroine who appears in the Euripidean play to which the American dramatist alludes in his notes. That man's will which enabled Clytemnestra to become an effective instrument of divine justice is incorporated in Lavinia's woodenly erect form. It is she, not the weak Orin, who plans the intrigue by means of which her brother is shown proof of Christine's deception and Adam Brant is murdered. (Although Orin pulls the trigger — even the method of murder is modernly indicated — it is largely at the instigation of his sister that he agrees to seek out the treachery. Once he has proof, instead of acting in full possession of his powers, he goes berserk.)

Lavinia is enslaved to the Aegisthus of the American drama through her love for him, a love that ultimately is to trap her into remaining a prisoner of the dead Mannons. Her intense hatred for her mother has its origin in Christine's ill treatment of her as a child. She was always regarded with disgust by her mother because she aroused memories of Ezra's ineptitude as a lover, and her daughter sensed the rejection. Unlike the reaction of the son to his father, the girl who is suffering from an Oedipus or Electra complex begins life with a normal amount of love for the mother, as Lavinia mentions. It is not until the girl transfers her love to her father that she experiences feelings of jealousy and hatred towards the mother. If Lavinia has made every effort to minimize her resemblance to her mother and has taken on the mannerisms of her father, it is because she had been rejected by one parent and exploited by the other. The feeling Ezra has for his daughter is love which has been rerouted after first being intended for his wife. Ezra is as much responsible for the complex from which Lavinia suffers as his wife is for Orin's neurosis.

Just as Orin considers Adam Brant a threat to his exclusive

hold on his mother's love, Lavinia has good reason to regard Christine as her rival, both for the father's affection that she has come to consider as her exclusive right and for the love of the man who resembles her father and possesses those attractive elements in his nature Ezra had suppressed. When Lavinia fails to succeed her mother in Brant's affections, she experiences once more that defeat occasioned by her father's resolution to embrace life and seek a healthier relationship with his wife and daughter. Only one course remains to her. She can avenge the loss of Ezra's love and succeed finally in destroying her hated rival by separating Christine from the two remaining men who love her. She causes Orin to become estranged from his mother and has him murder Brant.

When at last Lavinia feels liberated from the restraining influences of her past, it overtakes her. As she is accepting Peter's proposal of marriage, she makes a fatal slip and calls him Adam. Although she tries to confuse her beau by lying that she has heard the name only in the Bible, she cannot fool herself or the spectator. She renounces, with Peter, her last chance of earthly happiness and walks into the shrouded and deserted house to live the life of a recluse. Infinitely worse than death, her fate — the doom that awaits all Mannons — is to live out her life apart from all humanity. There is a good deal that is heroic in her final acceptance of that destiny: "I'll never go out or see anyone! I'll have the shutters nailed closed so no sunlight can ever get in. I'll live alone with the dead, and keep their secrets, and let them hound me, until the curse is paid out and the last Mannon is let die!" (866–67) The fact that she is the last Mannon involves more tragedy for Lavinia than is apparent on the surface. Her character is a complex one, and although she drives her brother to suicide, mainly through the power of suggestion, she does love him. After Orin has taunted her with the thought that he may die mysteriously, as his father before him, she cries out, "Don't keep saying that! . . . Don't you know I'm your sister, who loves you, who would give her life to bring you peace?" (843) Later on, she regrets having had thoughts of his death and she prays,

"Oh, God, don't let me have such thoughts! You know I love Orin! Show me the way to save him!" (845)

Praying to God, however, is futile because no God exists in this universe of Mannons. Indeed, the entire nation appears to be gripped by a sense of hopelessness. We hear of the assassination of President Lincoln. The sounds of mourning and grief, so familiar in the Mannon household, are echoed throughout the land. The only God is the wrathful, thunder and lightning deity of the Puritan meeting house, and the divine radiance which emanates from that source is somewhat less than benevolent. As Lionel Trilling has pointed out, there is no society either. Lavinia's pronouncement that "there is no one left to punish me . . . I've got to punish myself!" strikes him as "the final statement of a universe in which society has no part." He concludes that "the social organism has meant nothing." [30]

Only the chorus of townsfolk represents society, and we see such local types as Amos; Louisa; Mr. Hills, the minister and his wife; and Dr. Blake, the family physician, engaged primarily in spying upon and gossiping about the family's private affairs. They are narrow-minded, ignorant individuals who are incapable of understanding the many-faceted problems which confront the Mannons. And their view of love is best expressed by Dr. Blake, leering, smirking, and whispering his professional diagnosis that it was "love" that caused Ezra to have a heart attack. We are very far from the aid and comforts of Apollo, Athena, and the gentle Eumenides.

Both *La Machine infernale* and *Mourning Becomes Electra* focus on character. All action in the French drama is concerned with Oedipe's progression towards that moment when he confronts his true self and becomes, as the Voice proclaims, a man. Similarly, what we are concerned with in O'Neill's play is the personal cosmos of the Mannons. We see them destroying one another until the last Mannon must face the truth of her own makeup and expiate the crimes of the entire family. Motives are revealed and action is seen to follow. Along with the new emphasis on character comes a new view of characters.

The dilemmas in which they are involved are fundamentally private ones. We see them struggling with domestic problems. In *La Machine infernale* we are carried beyond the doors of the boudoir and witness an intimate moment between the newly wed Jocaste and Oedipe. (I cannot agree, however, with George Steiner that the scene is in bad taste.[31] The Freudian mechanisms are, perhaps, clumsily handled, for understatement is not one of the scene's virtues, but Cocteau has so altered the myth that the scene is not only in proper good taste but is, it seems to me, quite necessary.)

Also in *Mourning Becomes Electra* we have a bedroom scene between the modern Agamemnon and his Clytemnestra. The sentiments expressed between husband and wife on that occasion, however, are somewhat less than romantic. Their arguments become accusations and recriminations, culminating in Christine's poisoning Ezra. The tone here is closer to the Greek source than are the tender exchanges of Oedipe and Jocaste. One is reminded of the bitterness that existed between Agamemnon and Clytemnestra. All that O'Neill has done is to take his characters inside the house. In the treatment of the marriage itself, O'Neill is, possibly, taking the most modern approach. The author's presentation of domestic strife — a most Strindbergian presentation at that — and his sympathetic view of love which exists outside of marriage, coupled with the suggestion of divorce, is a new addition to the tale.

O'Neill concentrates on the family, its attitudes and behavioral patterns to create "psychological fate." He labors, often excessively, to infuse his work with a sense of impending disaster. Cocteau does not make the effort that the American does to create modern fate. He works with symbols, vague allusions to gods and an infernal machine, but his drama gives us a view of that same doom that befalls the Mannons.

O'Neill's tragic conception, unlike that of Cocteau, was such that the American house of Atreus is not destroyed because of the fact that its members submit to unconscious drives; the contrary is strongly indicated. The Mannons are destroyed because they resist their interior compulsions. The unconscious impulse is a romantic one, and it is a good one because through its realization one can find happiness. The family prospered in its early ship-building days. Environmental influences caused each Mannon to suppress his romantic impulses. (Suppression, unlike repression is a voluntary and consciously inhibitive act.) [32]

The American dramatist made more of an effort to keep his audience aware of the Freudian theory behind his creations than did Cocteau. Characters' motives, such as Christine's hatred of her husband, are made explicitly clear. The symbols used are relatively simple ones, and if we have any doubts that the American playwright intended the South Sea island of Orin's dream to represent prenatal bliss, for example, we have merely to look at O'Neill's notes to the play for reassurance (see note #30, p. 48). Finally, the climax of *Mourning Becomes Electra* is caused by a slip of the tongue, one of those Freudian "parapraxias" to which psychoanalysts often attach great meanings and to which the playwright attached great dramatic importance, for it is responsible for Lavinia's sudden and lasting confrontation with her past.

The situation for the individual is hopeless. He can appeal to no merciful force in the universe because none exists. There is no hope of reconciliation with a malicious god because no such deity is responsible for his fate. The surrounding society of which he is a distant member is cold and impersonal. He does not present his case before an impartial tribunal because, although he may be responsible for a crime, the fundamental issue is not one of justice. His dilemma is that his unconscious compulsions make it impossible for him to achieve a harmonious rapport with his environment. When, after stumbling blindly from one erroneous act to the next, he realizes that no aid is forthcoming from external sources and that he must look within himself for the answer to the riddle of his existence, he discovers that he possesses a nature which cannot be changed and that eternal defeat is his doom. Pitiful as he is, he shares with all great heroes a long-delayed but soundly acquired humility which makes it possible for him to bend his head and accept censure for his crimes, and therein lies his greatness. The censurer is himself. Awakening from their temporary illusory happiness, Oedipe and Lavinia have the capacity to impose upon themselves great suffering in order to atone for their misdeeds. They both reject the tempting peace of death and accept the unhappiness of which they are assured in life.

Another American dramatist who gained inspiration from a myth and concentrated on unconscious motivation in delineating character was Tennessee Williams. In *Orpheus Descending* (1957), his drama of doomed love in a small southern town, Williams reinterpreted the legend of Orpheus and Eurydice. Like O'Neill and Cocteau before him, Williams was intent on exploring the psychological pressures and frustrations that torment man. He found in the ancient material an occasion to reveal the interior lives of his contemporary figures. Employing the same technique as his predecessors, he searched for a universal element which would serve as a basis for his new creation. He found it in the fundamental themes of life and death. His play is enriched and shaped by the tale of the lovers who passed from the realm of the living to that of the dead and approached once more the world of light.

The hero of Williams' play is a young man named Val (short for Valentine) Xavier. He represents the famous poet and musician of the Greek myth. Instead of a lyre he carries a guitar, and he wears an unusual jacket, made of snakeskin, mottled white, black, and gray. His Eurydice is Lady Torrance and, unlike the legendary character, she is not married to Orpheus but to a man named Jabe Torrance, the owner of a general dry goods store. Fate placed Val in the small town in which we find him. Traveling through the area the day before, his car broke down in a storm and he was obliged to spend the night in the local jail. Seeking work, he is led into Lady's store by the Sheriff's wife. Vee Talbot, the woman who has helped him, believes that Jabe Torrance's wife can use some help about the place because her husband, gravely ill with cancer, is not expected to recover. Such is the event that initiates the surface story, a story that appears to be far removed from that of the legend. However, beneath the surface the structure of the myth can be perceived. The store, with its connecting "confectionery," into which Val is led is actually Hades. Like Hades it is divided into two parts: the dry goods section of the store, with its stairs leading up to Jabe's room, is cobwebbed and damp. This suggests Tartarus, the place of torment. The confectionery, glimpsed partly through a wide-arched door, is described as "shadowy and poetic." [33] Although it is to be described in greater detail as it takes on increased significance in later scenes, the confectionery represents something which is apparent in this first rescription. It represents a land of spring, song, and eternal happiness. The confectionery calls to mind the Elysian Fields. More evocative than precise, various symbols are scattered throughout the work.

The Pluto who holds sway in this underworld is the dying Jabe, and his wife — in addition to representing Eurydice — serves as his Persephone. Lady Torrance is an emotional female, whose Mediterranean origin is used by the dramatist to account for her hot blood. Exploding periodically and murmuring oaths in what one takes to be Sicilian dialect, she is a stereotype, the validity of which her creator apparently never questioned. Ignoring the fact that the same type (equally loud and panting) appears in *The Rose Tattoo*, where the mythical structure is not present, and ignoring, further, the possibility that this type is created by sheer coincidence, we will give Williams the benefit of the doubt and suggest that in noting his heroine's national origin he was influenced by the knowledge that Persephone was a Sicilian Greek, spirited away from her island home by the god of the dead.

Lady's marriage to Jabe, like that of Persephone, was a forced one; it was forced by the circumstances of her life. She lived with a father who made a living selling bootlegged wine and liquor to young couples who found a hideaway in the orchard he planted on a piece of property called Moon Lake. There, among white wooden arbors, the young people would do their courting, the background music of Neapolitan love ballads being provided by the Sicilian and his daughter. Business was booming, until Lady's father made a grave mistake. He sold liquor to Negroes. Incensed, the Mystic Crew (actually the Ku Klux Klan) burned to the ground the Moon Lake orchard, along with its owner. Alone and destitute, Lady accepted the financial security that Jabe offered her. The marriage, which is devoid of love, has failed; and all the town knows it. One observer, summing up the situation in homespun philosophical terms, is led to generalize: "People can live together in hate for a long time. . . ." (9) The pair, we hear, react to each other with "instant hostility." (24)

Mystery attaches to the rooms that Lady and her husband inhabit on top of the store. Lady objects to anyone "snoopin' aroun' upstairs." (5) However, one of the procession of neighbors who continually file into the store has not respected her privacy, and the woman reports: "They got two separate bedrooms which are not even connectin'. At opposite ends of the hall, and everything is so dingy an' dark up there. Y'know what it seemed like to me? A county jail!" (5) [34] The description of the living quarters calls to mind that Pluto's palace, deep within the underworld, was dark and gloomy, haunted by strange apparitions and surrounded by groves of somber trees. On the landing of the staircase leading to the bedrooms is "a sinister-looking palm tree in a greenish-brown jardiniere." (3)

The drama consists mainly of Val's interaction with the three women who come to know him: Lady; Carol Cutrere, the daughter of a declined aristocratic family; and Vee Talbot, the Sheriff's wife. Carol is modeled on Cassandra. Although she played no part in the tale of the Greek Orpheus and Eurydice, the character fulfills an important role in this drama. Carol has a disturbed sexual nature, as do the other two women. A nymphomaniac, she begins to make demands on Val from the moment she meets him, but the young man ignores her. And longing for understanding, Carol makes an attempt to reach him by explaining the factors that led to her decline. She was once, she relates, a vehement supporter of civil rights. In the cause of Negro freedom she humiliated herself and exhausted her financial resources, only to discover that she could not

combat the opposed majority. Admitting that she enjoyed exhibiting herself, besides having some sincere and noble ideals,
Carol was upset to find herself arrested on a charge of "lewd
vagrancy." Unable to stand the failure of her efforts and resentful at being rejected by her society, she decided to defy further
the people who were already looking at her with disdain. The
only emotional satisfaction she can enjoy now is going from one
affair to another and shocking the gossips around her. A somewhat ironic Cassandra, she speaks of contacting the spirits: "I
have a knock in my engine. It goes knock, knock, and I say
who's there. I don't know whether I'm in communication with
some dead ancestor or the motor's about to drop out and leave
me stranded in the dead of night on the Dixie Highway." (26)

Carol tells Val about a local pastime: making love among
the memorial stones on Cypress Hill, "the local bone orchard."
Here Williams may have had in mind the White Rock which,
on the outskirts of Hades, symbolized the bleaching skeletons
of the dead. Among the dead on Cypress Hill Carol communi-
cates most clearly, and she reveals to Val what the spirits say:
"They chatter together like birds on Cypress Hill, but all they
say is one word and that one word is 'live,' they say 'Live, live,
live, live, live!' It's all they've learned, it's the only advice they
can give. — Just live." (28)

There is something in Val's character that attracts Carol.
There is a wild freedom about him, symbolized by his snakeskin jacket, which corresponds to something within her own
spirit. Earlier she had approached a Negro "Conjure Man"
and requested that he demonstrate for her his celebrated talent
for sounding a Choctaw cry, "a series of barking sounds that
rise to a high sustained note of wild intensity." (16) As if in
response to that animal-like cry, Val had made his first entrance.
Carol fears that the town will attempt to curb his freedom and
thus destroy the young man.

Val-Orpheus is the young poet. Separated from those who
are unappreciative of the beauty he creates, he is an unsuccessful bard. He carries with him, as testimony of the insensitivity
of man, a letter of recommendation from a previous employer

which, in its candor, does him far more harm than good: "This boy worked for me three months in my auto repair shop and is a real hard worker and is good and honest but is a peculiar talker and that is the reason I got to let him go but would like to . . . keep him, Yours truly." (38) Just how "peculiar" his talk is becomes apparent when he defines his aspirations in life. Val would like to be able to imitate the actions of a bird he claims to have seen once:

> A kind of bird that don't have legs so it can't light on nothing but has to stay all its life on its wings in the sky. . . . [birds that] live their whole lives on the wing, and they sleep on the wind, that's how they sleep at night, they just spread their wings and go to sleep on the wind like other birds fold their wings and go to sleep on a tree. They sleep on the wind and never light on this earth but one time when they die! (41–2)

Val longs for a life untainted by the corruption of the earth. He has, in the past, led a lonely existence, and all contacts with people have proved unsatisfactory. Living alone on the bayou he was a child of nature. However, when he grew up and entered the city, he learned of evil: "I went to New Orleans in this snakeskin jacket. . . . It didn't take long for me to learn the score." (49) Being a handsome young fellow, much sought after by women, Val learned that he, too, like Lady, could sell himself. He has concluded that the world is made up of two types of individual: the buyer and the bought, and he tells Lady sadly, "We're all of us sentenced to solitary confinement inside our own skins, for life!" (49)

This Orpheus is a disillusioned poet. He is, of course, Tennessee Williams' particular poet. The man with the "wild beauty" about him must fight to preserve his freedom from the women who wish, like all women, to exert a sexual domination over the male. The image of the poet as great lover whose desire for freedom is thwarted by sex-starved women is one that Williams took from D. H. Lawrence, as Signi Falk has noted.[35] What is interesting about *Orpheus Descending* is the way in which the American dramatist used elements in the

Greek myth to reinforce his conception. The women who surround Val and make demands upon him (we have already discussed one of them) are the Maenads of the legend, the promiscuous followers of Dionysus who tore Orpheus limb from limb after he ignored their god, along with Artemis and — following the death of Eurydice — took to preaching the joys of homosexual love.

To what extent one may read veiled references to homosexuality in Val's description of his past is a matter of individual interpretation. It is significant that at present the young man has decided, having reached the age of thirty, that "shacking with strangers is okay for kids in their twenties," (22) and that whatever attempt he has made to break away from women in the past he will now apply himself to with increased vigor.

The woman who has conducted him into hell, Vee Talbot, is another female with whom he comes in contact. She makes no physical demands on him, but the two form a relationship which eventually brings about his destruction. Married to a sheriff who gets a sadistic pleasure out of violence, Vee has turned to artistic creation as a means of achieving emotional release. Her husband is so insensitive that he not only cannot understand her passion for painting, but he is equally inept at understanding her love of art in general. Vee turns to the young poet for understanding; she recognizes in him a kindred sensitive soul. When she tries to explain what her work means to her, Val replies, "You don't have to explain. I know what you mean. Before you started to paint, it didn't make sense." (66) "It" is existence. Vee lives through her painting. The violence she detests equals the corruption which Val is trying to rid himself of. In a gesture completely devoid of self-consciousness, Val lifts her hands from her lap and kisses them. As he does so, the Sheriff walks in and, as one would expect, interprets the action in the worst possible way.

With Lady Torrance, the woman with whom he becomes most involved, Val has something in common, too. Both, because of events that have occurred in their past, have become disillusioned with love. Val believes that everyone is waiting for some answer that will show life to have some sense. However, love is not the answer; he tells Lady: "That's the make-believe answer. It's fooled many a fool besides you an' me, that's the God's truth . . . ." (48) Lady is similarly bitter. Before her marriage to Jabe Torrance, she and Carol's brother, David Cutrere, were lovers. As a result of the affair, Lady had become pregnant. That summer two events occurred: her father lost his life and David left her to marry a wealthy woman. Without ever telling David about the baby, she had an abortion and later married Jabe. She has avoided David ever since, but during the course of the play's action he must come into the store to retrieve his sister, and a meeting is unavoidable. When they face one another, Lady — on an impulse — turns on him and tells him all. She forces him to admit that he has regretted rejecting her and now leads an unhappy existence. Lady relishes the revenge, "I hold hard feelings!" (62) She also makes the admission, common to one who has a great deal of pride and who has just made a confession involving her deepest feelings for another, "I made a fool of myself!" (63)

Val and Lady hardly resemble the legendary lovers at this point. Matters become worse when Lady offers Val the use of a bedroom-alcove, which is screened from the dry goods portion of the store by an Oriental drapery, the design of which is "a gold tree with scarlet fruit and fantastic birds." Val is hurt; once more he feels that a woman is trying to buy him. He characterizes Lady as "a not so young and not so satisfied woman that hired a man off the highway to do double duty without paying overtime for it. . . . I mean a store clerk days and a stud nights. . . ." (80) Although she strikes him, Lady is soon putting aside all her pride and screaming out, in Williams' huge capital letters, that she needs him to go on living. Lady, like the other women in Williams' play, is driven by erotic frustration, but she is also Eurydice, and she begins to fall in love with Val.

Gradually, that hesitancy that marked the couple's first awkward moments together begins to give way to a friendlier, more relaxed attitude. They reach the point where they can talk about themselves with honesty and maturity. Finally the disillusioned poet tells the woman, simply, "I feel a true love for you, Lady." (107) The story of the progress of that love is the dramatic account of the transformation of two bitter people, very much of the twentieth century, into the immortal lovers of the ancient tale. For in giving Lady his love, Val rescues her from the legal prostitution in which Jabe held her, and in fathering the child which Lady ecstatically announces she is about to have, after years of a childless marriage, Val gives her life and rescues her from the realm of the dead. The romance of the modern Orpheus and his Eurydice has progressed not against a background of Neapolitan love ballads, like that of the young couples of Moon Lake, but to the accompaniment of dull thuds. Above them in his palace-bedroom, Jabe continually knocks out a summons to Lady. Knocking, like the dead who knock to Carol as she drives along on the Dixie Highway, Jabe wishes to snatch his wife away from the life-bringer. Lady tells Val:

> Death's knocking for me! Don't you think I hear him, knock, knock, knock? It sounds like what it is! Bones knocking bones. . . . Ask me how it felt to be coupled with death up there, and I can tell you. My skin crawled when he touched me. But I endured it. I guess my heart knew that somebody must be coming to take me out of this hell! You did. You came. Now look at me! I'm alive once more! (109)

Val has followed Carol's advice that he live life to the fullest, but he has made one error. He has remained in hell. Worse still, he has put aside his snakeskin jacket and donned a conservative navy blue business suit, thus failing to heed the warning which the Cassandra of the drama brings him:

> You're in danger here, Snakeskin. You've taken off the jacket that said: 'I'm wild, I'm alone!' and put on the nice blue uniform of a convict! . . . Last night I woke up thinking about you again. I drove all night to bring you this warning of danger. . . . The message I came here to give you was a

> warning of danger! I hoped you'd hear me and let me take
> you away before it's too late. (59)

Val is surrendering to the life of the town. He has become a
prisoner of the Hades into which he has descended as surely as
the convicts of the nearby penitentiary. The townsmen who
fail to appreciate his sensitivity threaten his creative life. Their
threat results from their jealousy of the only aspect of his creative powers to which they are sensitive, his virility. Henry
Popkin has pointed out that the guitar which the modern Orpheus carries in lieu of a lyre — a guitar which is covered with
the signatures of the immortals of the jazz world — is a phallic
symbol. In the scene in which the disturbed Sheriff accuses
Val of making advances towards his wife, the sexually unsuccessful men approach the young poet with knives drawn as if
to castrate him.[36] The castration threat is Tennessee Williams'
interpretation of one force which perils Orpheus in Pluto's
realm. The hero of the American drama is less fortunate than
his Greek counterpart. He never emerges from Hades.

Lady must perform one final act. She has planned to
reopen the confectionery; decorating the room herself. She has
transformed it into a replica of the vineyard at Moon Lake, for
she has discovered that it was Jabe who led the crew that destroyed the original orchard, and she refuses to leave until her
husband sees a festive reopening take place. Because she
blames him for the death of her father, her death, and the
death of her unborn child, she wants him to see the vineyard
come alive while he is dying. The orchard has stood as a symbol of life throughout the drama; as we noted previously, it was
there that young lovers (Lady and David among them) would
gather in the spring. By destroying it, Jabe was able to claim
his wife. Now, by creating a vineyard of paper, by hanging
artificial branches of blooming fruit trees, Lady has been able
to recreate a land which contrasts with Jabe's Tartarus. The
confectionery — more apparently now — is the Elysian Fields.

As Lady is joyfully telling Val about her plans, Jabe's nurse
enters. Displaying something less than scientific detachment,

she looks from Lady to Val with a knowing glance and confirms
the woman's pregnancy. Eurydice becomes Williams' predatory
female again. She tells Val that he can leave now, for he has
given her life and she no longer needs him. In a burst of triumph she dashes up to the landing and, blowing a paper horn
she has taken from the confectionery, announces, "I've won,
I've won, Mr. Death, I'm going to bear!" (114) In response, the
pallid Jabe appears. Clutching the trunk of the false palm tree
with one hand, he fires a revolver with the other. He hits Lady,
who had rushed to shield Val's body with her own (for it seems
that she loves the poet after all). And Death repossesses Eurydice. For Val she has represented an ideal, unattainable and
fleeting, as is the ideal for which the poet strives. Vowing that
he will have Val burned, as he burned Lady's father, Jabe
shouts out that his clerk has killed his wife and is robbing his
store.

The violent ending in which Val is killed by the mob of
townsmen combines two versions of the legend's end. Indicating that the men have gotten hold of a blowtorch, the dramatist recalls the account which relates that Orpheus, who had
divulged divine secrets, was killed by Zeus who struck him with
a thunderbolt. Also suggested, by the sound of a dog baying
and an earlier incident in the drama in which we hear of pursuing hounds overtaking and killing an escaped convict, Val is
torn apart limb from limb, like the Orpheus who was similarly
destroyed by the Maenads. Here, the murderers are not
Maenads, for these figures have done with Val. The dogs are
driven by a lynch mob led by the Sheriff. There is particular
irony in this, especially when one thinks of certain elements in
the myth. When Orpheus reached the gates of Pluto's abode,
he encountered Cerberus, the three-headed dog with the ser-
pent tail. The watchdog was friendly enough to spirits enter-
ing, but allowed no one to depart. In Hades, too, Orpheus came
upon the three judges: Minos, Æacus, and Rhadamanthus, who
assigned the souls of the dead to one of the two regions of the
lower world. The Greek bard had so charmed judges and dog
that he was allowed to enter and depart freely. Val's inability

to charm the Sheriff and his pack is an ironic parallel to the myth and a double commentary on the destruction of the sensitive by the insensitive and on the nature of Southern lynch-mob justice!

Despite those instances when Val's experience runs contrary to that of Orpheus, he has journeyed the same route taken by the Greek hero. He has descended into hell; given new life to the woman he loves; and, on the brink of saving her, he has lost her. Upon this bare skeleton Williams has built a drama of life in a bigoted, cancerous community. He has adjusted the plot and the setting, and he has added new characters to the old legend. The result is a work which marks an advance in Williams' work, for as critic Richard Watts, Jr. has pointed out, the playwright has given us a broad panorama of the harshness and cruelty of the world that destroys its poets:

> By characterizing the small Southern community in which his sympathetic characters live, and letting us observe something of the malice, intolerance, and social and moral decadence that drove them to their doom, he has provided an additional ring of brutal truth and given a new dimension to his tragedy.[37]

The enlarged view results, in part, from Williams' musings over his mythological material, for it soon becomes evident that his thoughts about the torments of hell have influenced him to conclude that hell overwhelms the Torrance store as it does Two River County and even New Orleans. Hell becomes all of society.

The play has a number of weaknesses. Most important, the myth of Orpheus and Eurydice which Williams uses to shape his work is superimposed on his original conception. The modern work does not grow out of the ancient legend, and the symbolism is often involved and confused. Where a classical parallel does not serve his purpose, Williams makes frequent use of Christian parallels and does not hesitate to mix parallels and symbols. Thus Lady represents both Eurydice and the Virgin Mary at the same time. It is unquestionable, nevertheless, that the addition of mythological material does enrich the final work. Desirous of portraying the psychological pressures and frustrations which plague men, Williams turns to the ancient legend in an effort to remind us that he deals with the most basic themes of life. If the story that he gives us is often sordid and violent, it is also a tragic tale of great universal significance. It tells us, like the story which it calls to mind, that life is fleeting, and happiness — like men — shortlived. It mourns wasted opportunities and the tragedy of a lost second chance. Above all, it urges us to heed the advice of the prophetic Carol, "Catch at whatever comes near you, with both your hands, until your fingers are broken." (21)

## ✻ NOTES

[1] The influence of Freud has been so extensive that the term "Freudian" is used as a general identification for the collective contributions of Jung, Adler, and others, who hold many views in common with Freud; the term is so used in this study.

[2] Claire Russell and W. M. S. Russell, *Human Behavior* (Boston: Little, Brown & Co., 1961), p. 384.

[3] Otto Rank, *The Trauma of Birth* (New York: Robert Brunner, 1952), p. 187.

[4] *Ibid.*, p. 188.

[5] *Ibid.*, pp. 165–66.

[6] *Ibid.*, p. 143.

[7] Jean Cocteau, *La Machine infernale* (Paris: Bernard Grasset, 1934), p. 15. All subsequent page references to this edition will be given immediately after the quotation. All translations of quotations taken from the individual plays discussed throughout this study are those of the author of the study.

[8] Rank, *op. cit.*, pp. 144–45.

[9] Earlier, when the Sphinx strokes the neck of the young child who appears with his mother, the child asks, "Mother, is this woman the Sphinx?"

[10] Neal Oxenhandler, *Scandal & Parade: The Theater of Jean Cocteau* (New Brunswick: Rutgers University Press, 1957), p. 144.

[11] Francis Fergusson, *The Idea of a Theater* (Princeton: Princeton University Press, 1949), p. 202.

[12] Rank, *op. cit.*, p. 98.

[13] Rank, *op. cit.*, p. 196.

[14] Fergusson, *op. cit.*, p. 16.

[15] Jean Boorsch, "The Use of Myths in Cocteau's Theater," *Yale French Studies*, No. 5 (1950), p. 79.

[16] George Steiner, *The Death of Tragedy* (New York: Alfred A. Knopf, Inc., 1961), p. 330.

[17] Eugene O'Neill, "Working Notes and Extracts from a Fragmentary Work Diary" in *European Theories of the Drama: With a Supplement on the American Drama*, ed. Barrett H. Clark (New York: Crown Publishers, Inc., 1947), p. 535.

[18] Doris M. Alexander, "Psychological Fate in *Mourning Becomes Electra*," *PMLA*, LXVIII (Dec., 1953), p. 933.

[19] *Ibid.*, pp. 923–34.

[20] Doris Falk, *Eugene O'Neill and the Tragic Tension* (New Bruns-

wick: Rutgers University Press, 1958), p. 189.

[21] O'Neill, "Working Notes and Extracts from a Fragmentary Work Diary," p. 533.

[22] Eugene O'Neill, *Mourning Becomes Electra* in *Nine Plays* (New York: Random House, Inc., 1954), p. 689. All subsequent page references to this edition will be given immediately after the quotation.

[23] O'Neill, "Working Notes and Extracts from a Fragmentary Work Diary," p. 535.

[24] Oscar Cargill first notes the double motivation of O'Neill's Electra in *Intellectual America* (New York: The Macmillan Co., 1941), p. 714.

[25] O'Neill, "Working Notes and Extracts from a Fragmentary Work Diary," p. 531.

[26] See O'Neill, "Working Notes and Extracts from a Fragmentary Work Diary," p. 533.

[27] Cargill, *op. cit.*, pp. 716–17.

[28] O'Neill, "Working Notes and Extracts from a Fragmentary Work Diary," p. 530.

[29] Cargill, *op. cit.*, p. 717.

[30] Lionel Trilling, "The Genius of O'Neill," *O'Neill and His Plays*, ed. Oscar Cargill, N. Bryllion Fagin, and William J. Fisher (New York: New York University Press, 1961), p. 299.

[31] Steiner, *op. cit.*, p. 327.

[32] The distinction is Freud's.

[33] Tennessee Williams, *Orpheus Descending: Battle of Angels* (New York: James Laughlin, 1958), p. 3. All subsequent page references to this edition will be given immediately after the quotation.

[34] The minor female characters function as a somewhat informal chorus. They represent the community of gossips who express their shock at the main characters' defiance of the community norms. Sometimes they turn upon one another. One instance occurs when one of the Temple sisters, representing the genteel tradition of the old aristocratic South — that tradition of breeding, good taste, and the hospitality afforded in lovely old plantation homes boasting exquisite Greek porticos — turns to her sister and remarks of two neighbors who have just departed, "Both those wimmen are as common as dirt." (30)

[35] Signi L. Falk, *Tennessee Williams* (New York: Twayne Publishers, Inc., 1961), p. 164.

[36] Henry Popkin, "The Plays of Tennessee Williams," *The Tulane Drama Review*, IV (Spring, 1960), p. 60

[37] Richard Watts, Jr., "Orpheus Descending," *Theatre Arts*, XLII (Sept., 1958), pp. 25–6.

# ※ II

## ※ Religious and Philosophical Ideas

If mythological material in the Oedipus, Orestes, and Orpheus legends provided dramatists like Jean Cocteau, Eugene O'Neill, and Tennessee Williams with characters, themes, and symbols useful in developing a view of man as psychologically driven, the accounts of heroes like Orestes have also been valuable as a source of inspiration to playwrights presenting a view of man consciously and freely choosing a course of action. O'Neill may have considered Orestes a neurotic weakling in love with his mother and jealous of his father, but Harry, Lord Monchensey, the Orestes of T. S. Eliot's *The Family Reunion* (1939), seems to voice his creator's convictions when he states emphatically.

It is not my conscience,
Not my mind, that is diseased, but the world I have to live in.[1]

The exploration of Harry's world and the hero's self-definition within his world are what form the substance of Eliot's play. One can explain much of what has happened to Harry by referring to whatever the psychoanalyst knows about human behavior, but the dramatist refrains from doing so himself. Rather, he reworks the ancient story of divine retribution to heighten its religious significance and explain certain complexities of life from the viewpoint of a twentieth-century Christian. Eliot structured his play so that the return of the hero, his twenty-four hour stay at home, and his departure form the entire drama. Events that have occurred prior to Harry's homecoming are recalled through conversations with other characters. Action suffers, for what transpires during the drama, symmetrically divided into two acts of three scenes each, is mainly talk, but the talking reveals the thematic parallels to the myth.

One aspect of the myth that most interested Eliot, as it did Eugene O'Neill, was the idea of the past exerting an influence upon the present, for he considered the past an essential part of the totality which is time. Time, Eliot believed, has a direction, and the past initiates time's inevitable journey. What was useful about the myth was that it presented certain facts, events, and themes, which, while they developed a basically deterministic view of life, could be valuable — if reinterpreted to suit the author's frame of reference — in expressing his own Christian views.

The experience of the mythological Orestes is essentially that of a man who has rejoined his community after years in exile and who, following an inevitable course prescribed by the curse, performs an act which at the same time that it satisfies the requirements of one segment of his society and one group of deities violates other human and divine laws. The opposing deities are eventually reconciled and Orestes is reconciled with them and is restored all his social rights and moral integrity.

Eliot has created a hero who is separated from his God because of sin. Just as Orestes moves from exile to reunion with his people and from alienation to reconciliation with the gods, Harry progresses from spiritual exile to reconciliation with his Creator. What differs in Eliot's conception is the meaning that he attaches to exile and reconciliation. The supernatural, or eternal, exists alongside the world of nature, or time, Eliot believes. Harry's acceptance of a way of life that leads him to spiritual reconciliation and self-definition is seen by the dramatist to be an acceptance of one view of time.

Various ways of conceiving time are represented by the other characters in the play, who hold opposing views and thereby are in conflict with each other. Eliot may alter the motives behind the opposition, but he retains the conflict for his dramatic purposes.

Harry returns to Wishwood, his ancestral home in northern England, in a state of extreme anguish. He has been living the life of an exile for the past eight years. Eliot gives us an account of his travels ( the Java Straits, Europe, and so on) to emphasize the restless existence he has led. However, his physical exile is merely an outward sign of a deeper, spiritual exile. Harry describes it to Agatha:

> At the beginning, eight years ago,
> I felt, at first, that sense of separation,
> Of isolation unredeemable, irrevocable —
> It's eternal, or gives a knowledge of eternity,
> Because it feels eternal while it lasts. That is one hell.
> Then the numbness came to cover it — that is another —
> That was the second hell of not being there,
> The degradation of being parted from my self (96)

Harry is being pursued by the equivalent of the Erinyes. Tormented by a wife he did not love, Harry wished for her death. The unfortunate woman subsequently obliged him, for what must have been the first time in their life together, by disappearing over the side of a liner transporting them across the Atlantic, although Harry seems to have difficulty deciding whether or not he actually pushed his wife overboard — the same difficulty that has bothered many critics.

What is clear from the viewpoint of a Christian is that the intention of an act has as much of a moral value as the act itself. Although the meaning of "murder" in the context of the play is closer to the concept of unhappiness in marriage than it is to the concept of killing, as critic John Peter has pointed out,[2] Harry has sinned because of his wish.

It is interesting that Harry is thirty-five years old, the symbolic age of Dante when he journeyed through the "selva oscura" towards God. Harry is in a symbolic hell. The hell is one conceived by a Christian because what Harry suffers from is a lack of knowledge that, ultimately, may be interpreted as an ignorance of God's true nature. Burdened with sin, he is denied the sight of God. Harry's torment will be at an end the moment that he is reunited with his true family, and his exile is finally ended. But such a resolution occurs gradually. Eliot's hero must make a number of important discoveries.

The chorus of uncles and aunts, which differs from the traditional Greek chorus because it does not comment upon the action, is generally indifferent to Harry's plight. His family is best represented by Violet, who confesses, "I do not understand/A single thing that's happened." (122) However, the aunts and uncles are useful, for along with Agatha and Amy they help to define Eliot's conception of time. The view that they support falls somewhat short of the vision that Harry is to embrace. The following quotation illustrates their feelings:

> I am afraid of all that has happened, and of all that is to come;
> Of the things to come that sit at the door, as if they had been there always.
> And the past is about to happen, and the future was long since settled.
> And the wings of the future darken the past. . . . (67)

They reveal that time has a cyclical pattern. The past gives way to the present, which gives way to the future, which becomes the past again. It is an endless flux. Eliot has Heraclitus in mind at this point, as he does in the climactic second act scene of *The Family Reunion,* when Agatha tells Harry:

> We do not pass twice through the same door
> Or return to the door through which we did not pass. (105)

Agatha is paraphrasing Heraclitus, "We do not step twice into the same river." However, if time is only this endless flux, existing independent of any permanence by which to anchor itself, then it has no meaning. Every moment is lost to the next. In an ethical sense, the sins of the past cannot be redeemed. Atonement is not possible. Such is Harry's torment. He describes himself:

> I am the old house
> With the noxious smell and the sorrow before morning
> In which all past is present, all degradation
> Is unredeemable. (28)

Despite his confusion, Harry has perceived a glimmer of the truth he seeks, and Agatha, the Cassandra of the play, notices it. She tells him,

>             . . . you only hold a fragment of the explanation
> It is only because of what you do not understand
> That you feel the need to declare what you do
> There is more to understand: hold fast to that
> As the way to freedom. (31)

The fragment of explanation that Harry possesses is not enough to help him and he takes a wrong turn. He attempts to escape the unredeemed past by searching out and living a past which never occurred. Harry returns to Wishwood — and here Eliot deviates from the traditional plot — not to avenge his father's death, but to find out what kind of man his father was and what kind of man he could have become had he remained at home. The search is for identity.

The dramatist alludes to a short story by Henry James, "The Jolly Corner," which relates the experience of Spencer Brydon, an expatriate American who, after having lived in Europe for the past thirty-three years of his life, returns to the New York home of his childhood. (James refers to his sojourn abroad as his "exile.") Walking through the empty rooms of the old house, Brydon seeks his alter ego, the man he would have become had he not had the experience of Europe. One can only guess at the nature of the impact of this story upon the expatriate Eliot. What is certain is that his hero, like James' hero, seeks to confront his possible past, and, in Harry's case, hopes to find refuge within that sphere of foresworn possibilities.

Harry's confrontation with Mary is just such an attempt
to snatch at an unheeded past possibility in order to overcome
present difficulty. Mary is patterned on Electra. An unwed
cousin, she has remained at Wishwood, suffering the domination of Harry's mother, Amy. She and Harry had been play-
mates as children. When they meet again, after years of separation, they are awkward and shy as they confront one another.
Mary's uneasiness is increased by the knowledge that it is part
of Amy's plan that she one day marry the heir to Wishwood.
The discomfort of the moment is keen and Mary begs off with
the excuse that she must change for dinner. However, Harry
pleads, "No, don't go just yet." (51) Harry wants to talk about
his childhood, and the true recognition occurs when they begin
to exchange memories of their secret hiding places where they
had shared childish adventures and found moments of happiness. The children, Harry and Mary, sought to escape from the
rest of the family. They had fashioned a block house in a hollow tree from which they fought the "Indians," who were
Harry's brothers, Arthur and John. When they returned home
late at night and were punished by the adults, they consoled
themselves with the thought that "they never found the secret."
(53) Eventually, however, "they" did find out, for when Harry
came home from school during the holidays and, after dispensing with the formal greetings, made his escape down to the
river to the old hiding place, he discovered that the tree had
been felled and a neat summer-house erected for the children.
Harry admits,

> It's absurd that one's only memory of freedom
> Should be a hollow tree in a wood by the river. (53)

And it is just that image of freedom which Harry pursues at
this point. With Mary lies the possibility of recapturing those
childhood moments of happiness and escape. She represents the
possible past. Desperately unhappy, Harry reaches a low ebb
in this scene and, describing his feelings, he seems to echo the
famous line of the fourth Canto of Dante's "Inferno," "*sanza
speme vivemo in disio*," when he tells her, "You do not know

what hope is until you have lost it." (54) For a brief moment, Mary appears to offer him hope. She offers him understanding and human love. With her he can live the life he missed. In a burst of optimism, he cries,

> You bring me news
> Of a door that opens at the end of a corridor,
> Sunlight and singing; when I had felt sure
> That every corridor only led to another,
> Or to a blank wall . . . . (59)

To recapture the past as one's possible life is to forego responsibility for the sins one has committed in the actual past. To speculate about what might have been is not to seek redemption but to seek solace from reality, for during those moments of speculation the actual past is forgotten. As Eliot affirms in the first stanza of "Burnt Norton,"

> What might have been is an abstraction
> Remaining a perpetual possibility
> Only in a world of speculation.[3]

No sooner does Harry acknowledge the value of Mary's feelings for him (for she does love him) than he is shocked to see the Eumenides take form before him. They have been pursuing him, but this is the first time that they appear before him at Wishwood, and Harry can only cry, "Oh, why now?" (59)

Harry has erred. Agatha — like her Greek counterpart, Cassandra — is keenly perceptive and even prophetic. She alone, in the midst of the obtuse family, knows what Harry's course will be, and she alone knows from the beginning why his homecoming will be painful. She explains,

> I mean painful, because everything is irrevocable,
> Because the past is irremediable,
> Because the future can only be built
> Upon the real past. (17)

The family ignores her — as Cassandra was ignored.

What Harry must do is forego the possible past and accept

the real past, with all its sins, before he can be free. Georges
Poulet has made some illuminating comments regarding Eliot's
view of time which help explain what Harry's course must be.
Comparing Eliot's search for lost time with that of Marcel
Proust, Poulet notes:

> A new time is revealed which is no longer the furious move-
> ment by which, in order more easily to possess the future, the
> present disencumbers itself of the past, but the reflective mo-
> tion by which, resigning itself to not existing by itself, the
> present concentrates upon the actions necessary to assure the
> preservation and the transmission of the past.
>
> But from this fact a new character of the past is revealed.
> It is its integrality. To decide to transmit the past to the future
> is to decide to transmit to the future *all* the past. . . . Accept-
> ance of the past does not solely imply the acceptance of its
> virtues, but also its sins. . . . To accept the past is to accept
> the burden of its sins and the necessity for their expiation. It
> is to accept time with all its consequences.
>
> Thus the new time takes on a significance no less tragic
> than the former time. For the tragedy of discontinuous mo-
> ments there is substituted the tragedy of a time that is ineluct-
> ably continuous.[4]

From Poulet's analysis it is clear that Eliot pondered long over
the significance of the past. In the Orestes tale, with its stress
on the effect of past transgressions upon present and future
human behavior, Eliot found an ideal parallel to his belief that
past sins remain unredeemed until the individual burdens himself with their expiation. Original sin, transmitted from generation to generation is, in *The Family Reunion,* the equivalent
for the curse on the House of Atreus. Harry's father, the first
Lord Monchensey that we hear of, succumbed to sin and error
by committing adultery with his wife's sister, Agatha, and by
willing his wife's death. Sin is compounded upon sin when
Harry, as Maud Bodkin has noted, repeats his father's sin by
following his unfortunate precedent and wishing for the death
of his own wife.[5]

Harry's rehabilitation begins the moment that he turns from the possible past and begins to seek the real past. His search begins with Dr. Warburton. The old family doctor belongs to Harry's childhood, as does Mary, but Warburton recalls memories of restraining influences, memories of Amy. He tells Harry,

> But you can't have forgotten
> The day when you came back from school with measles
> And we had such a time to keep you in bed.
> You didn't like being ill in the holidays. (64)

Warburton's association with Harry's family makes him a reliable witness to past events. He keeps the memory of the family sin alive. His efforts to discourage Harry from seeking the truth only add to the suspense. When Harry tries to find out what the doctor knows about his father, Warburton tells him:

> You know that your mother
> And your father were never very happy together:
> They separated by mutual consent
> And he went to live abroad. You were only a boy
> When he died. You would not remember. (74)

Harry replies, "But now I do remember." (74) Harry resolves to learn more and so he goes to Agatha.

In talking to his aunt, Harry begins to discover the significance of his return. He admits,

> Here I have been finding
> A misery long forgotten, and a new torture,
> The shadow of something behind our meagre childhood.
> Some origin of wretchedness. (97)

The wretchedness has its origin in his father's sin. An author of "simple plots" to murder his wife, the elder Lord Monchensey was dissuaded from carrying out his plans by Agatha, who acted for the sake of the unborn child Amy was carrying. The child was Harry, and Agatha tells him, "I felt that you were in

some way mine!" In discovering the origin of the family wretchedness, Harry learns something of his father's true nature.
Agatha describes him:

> Your father might have lived — or so I see him —
> An exceptionally cultivated country squire,
> Reading, sketching, playing on the flute,
> Something of an oddity to his county neighbors,
> But not neglecting public duties.
> He hid his strength beneath unusual weakness (98)

Agatha's disclosures of his father's unhappiness and the motives that drove him to sin provide Harry with a greater understanding both of his father and of himself. D. W. Harding has
pointed out that Harry's increased knowledge concerning the
truth of the miserable relations between his mother and father
"releases" him from his mother's domination.[6] Harding, I think,
stresses a psychological attachment between Harry and his
mother that Eliot would reject.[7] However, he is quite accurate
in noting the connection between Agatha's revelations and
Harry's subsequent conversion. Harry tells Agatha:

> I only now begin to have some understanding
> Of you, and of all of us. Family affection
> Was a kind of formal obligation, a duty
> Only noticed by its neglect. One had that part to play. (103)

Formal obligation stifled spontaneous love. What was wrong
with the marriage of Harry's parents — and with his own —
was that "there was no ecstasy." (98) As Amy dominated his
father, so did his wife dominate him. The little we know about
Harry's marriage comes from the testimony of Downing, who
characterizes Harry's wife as a demanding woman:

> It's my opinion that man and wife
> Shouldn't see too much of each other, Sir.
> Quite the contrary of the usual opinion,
> I dare say. She wouldn't leave him alone.
> And there's my complaint against these ocean liners
> With all their swimming baths and gymnasiums

There's not even a place where a man can go
For a quiet smoke, where the woman can't follow him.
She wouldn't leave him out of her sight. (40)

The "ecstasy" lacking in both marriages is that spiritual
love that is found in moments of contact with the divine.
Harry's realization of his father's situation is the first step on
his path to reconciliation with God. He comes to understand,
through Agatha, that time is not merely an endless flux. There
are moments, such as that "present moment of pointed light"
(99) when Harry's father and his aunt expressed their love,
that point to something beyond time. Such a moment of personal happiness is somewhat complex. In its essential meaning
it refers beyond the personal to all humanity. The moment is
the point of contact between time and eternity around which
the entire spatio-temporal order of nature arranges itself. The
concept is not a simple one and Agatha struggles to explain it
to Harry. Eliot resorts to the symbol of the rose garden here, for
it is in the rose garden where nature reveals to man something
beyond itself. Leonard Unger has discussed the significance of
the symbol in Eliot's work, and he notes that in *The Family
Reunion* it is Agatha who leads Harry to the door of the rose-
garden.[8] Eliot gives dramatic expression to the idea by having
the ecstatic moment occur as Harry realizes that Agatha, Amy's
rival, is his spiritual mother, and because super-reality has
greater truth than reality, Agatha is his true mother. Harry proclaims, "I feel happy for a moment, as if I had come home."
(102)

At the conclusion of Orestes' story, the curse has run its
course. And at this moment of climax in *The Family Reunion*,
Agatha realizes that the effect of sin in Lord Monchensey's family will expire:

O my child, my curse
You shall be fulfilled:
The knot shall be unknotted
And the crooked made straight. (107)

Time, then, does have a direction. It leads to God. Just as

Orestes achieves expiation for his crimes, Harry's sins will be redeemed. However, where in the original story Orestes is acquitted because of the intercession of Athena — and thus performs no act of his own to escape from his dilemma — Eliot presents the expiation as an act of human will illuminated by divine grace. Harry's spiritual exile is at an end when he realizes that "everything tends toward reconciliation." (101)

The progress of Eliot's hero has shared the rhythm of the cyclical pattern of nature: Death is followed by rebirth. The ethical significance of moments such as that shared with Agatha is the realization of the need for atonement. The philosophical theme that "the beginning and the end are common" [9] pervades the drama. The reconciliation which Orestes achieved is interpreted by Eliot to be a rebirth of soul. Harry returns to Wishwood, that is, to the beginning, severs ties with his natural mother, and is reunited with his spiritual mother and the entire spiritual world. Agatha explains.

> This way the pilgrimage
> Of expiation
> Round and round the circle
> Completing the charm
> So the knot be unknotted
> The crossed be uncrossed
> The crooked be made straight
> And the cures be ended (131)

As Agatha chants these words, she and Mary circle the birthday cake (which is also a circle).[10] The end that Harry is striving towards, which is God, completes the cycle of his life, for his beginning was his creation by God.

In following the Eumenides, an action which is very much outside the order of the myth, Harry is beginning a new life of self-sacrifice and contemplation. Such is the path towards the goal he seeks. Such, in fact, is the goal of every Christian hero of whom Harry is an example. That T. S. Eliot could have developed elements in classical literature and turned them to his own purposes is due, of course, to his great love of classical

literature and to his desire to communicate his vision through
his art. Always seeking parallels to the hero he continued to
create, he found Christian elements in the *Aeneid*. Speaking of
Aeneas' experience he notes:

> Aeneas' end is only a new beginning; and the whole point of
> the pilgrimage is something which will come to pass for future
> generations. His nearest likeness is Job, but his reward is not
> what Job's was, but is only in the accomplishment of his des-
> tiny. He is, in fact, the prototype of a Christian hero. For he
> is, humbly, a man with a mission; and the mission is every-
> thing.[11]

The time of the play's action is late March, and repeated
allusions to the death of the old year and the birth of spring
have led one critic to the conclusion that Eliot had the pattern
of the ritual plot in mind. Identifying Harry-Orestes as a representative of the new year and Amy-Clytemnestra as the corrupt
Earth Mother figure, Carol H. Smith maintains that

> the conflict between Harry and his mother . . . is patterned
> on the ritual plot with its agon between the sin-laden and im-
> potent representative of the old year and the reborn and sin-
> free god of the new year.[12]

The parallel is a tempting one, but the difficulty is that it ob-
scures the Christian meanings. In order for Harry to be reborn
"sin-free," he must first be sinful, and the conflict between
Harry and his mother does in fact exist before his rebirth. If a
good deal is said throughout the play about March and spring
it is because nature (like time) has a cyclical pattern which
merely repeats a progression: birth, decay, and death. For
Harry, however, the end, which is death, is the beginning of
immortal life.[13]

The worsening relations between Harry and his mother are
a reflection of the conflict between Orestes and Clytemnestra.
In *The Family Reunion,* the conflict is an ethical one and it
results from opposing views of time. The pattern of time which
Harry accepts carries with it certain ethical applications. Hu-

man life arranges itself around the moments of contact between nature and the supernatural, around the moments of absolute reality. The life of the spirit conquers time (that is, human time as opposed to spiritual time) by perceiving the absolute consciousness of absolute reality. When life is not centered around these moments, it is disordered. Such life is lived only in time, without reference to anything beyond it. It is lived according to the clock. Eliot tells us in "The Dry Salvages,"

> The tolling bell
> Measures times not our time.[14]

"Our" time is Harry's time. Life lived according to the clock stops when the clock stops. Amy leads such a life. She sounds her own death knell with the words, "The clock has stopped in the dark!" (126) Amy's delusion has been that she could impose a pattern of her own on the disordered flux which is human or clock time. She tries to do so by arresting time and imposing her own plans upon the future.

It is in attempting to arrange Harry's life that Amy meets the greatest frustration of all her hopes. Her plans included providing him with a docile wife, Mary. (The kind of tyranny Amy exerts over Eliot's Electra, the girl who has remained a member of her household during Harry's absence, is that of a rich relative who holds out the promise of an advantageous marriage.) However, as we have noted, Mary's comfort is insufficient to bring Harry any peace, and in rejecting her he dashes Amy's hopes for the marriage. And it is when he leaves his mother to pursue his own vision that Harry shatters all of Amy's plans for the future. Warned by Dr. Warburton that the shock would be too much for her old and feeble heart, he nonetheless leaves and Amy dies. The "murder" of his mother differs from Orestes' killing of Clytemnestra, but it is, as was the murder in the mythological tale, an expression of rejection. Harry rejects his natural mother in rejecting her way of life. Through Agatha he discovers his father.

Amy's domination of her husband is another example of

her attempt to order the present with a view towards ordering the future. Amy's description of her married life is acrid:

> Seven years I kept him,
> For the sake of the future, a discontented ghost,
> In his own house. What of the humiliation,
> Of the chilly pretences in the silent bedroom,
> Forcing sons upon an unwilling father?
> Dare you think what that does to one? (113)

It does nothing, apparently, to Amy, for Agatha notes,

> I know one thing, Amy;
> That you have never changed. (113)

The unhappiness resulting from this sad state of affairs does do something to her husband. The opposition which exists between Harry's father and mother is a reflection of the antagonism between Agamemnon and Clytemnestra; the antagonism between the modern couple results from Amy's way of life. Although Amy does not pick up an axe and actually murder her husband, she is responsible for turning him into "a discontented ghost." After the birth of the third child, the rupture in their marriage becomes permanent. Harry's father goes off to live the life of an exile (just as his son does years later) and eventually dies abroad. And as Clytemnestra is responsible for Cassandra's death, Amy's refusal to relinquish her husband to Agatha condemns her sister to a similarly tragic fate — "thirty years of solitude."

Harry has been aided on his journey by his aunt, Agatha. As "the other woman" Agatha comes between Amy and her husband and creates a grievance as damaging in its effect upon Amy as that created by the liaison between the Trojan princess and Agamemnon upon the resentful Clytemnestra. Amy blames Agatha for the failure of her marriage, but Agatha's defense rings true. She tells her sister, "What did I take? nothing that you ever had." (112) Eliot has altered the relationship between his Agamemnon and his Cassandra. Agatha is more suited to be the wife of Harry's father than is Amy. Agatha appears to be only an efficient principal of a woman's college, but her rather uncomplicated surface masks "a deeper organization." It is not simply that she "understands" Harry's father where his wife does not; she perceives the destructive element in Amy. Agatha knows that Amy's domination of her husband ruined him and that the love she offered him was the one bright moment in his life. Similarly, she is keen to Amy's efforts to dominate her son, and her love for Harry is such that she considers him her own.

There is a dilemma in *The Family Reunion* inspired by Orestes' dilemma, which results from the fulfillment of certain divine dictates and the rebellion against others. Harry's sin and that of his father is sin against the holy state of wedlock, a state consecrated by God. However, that the two states we hear of in the play were considerably less than perfect is due to the fact that the wives' behavior towards the husbands was un-Christian. In attempting to order their husbands' lives, Amy and Harry's wife usurped God's powers. Thus, in order to fulfill themselves and accept the divine plan in the universe, the men sin. However, the dilemma is solved because sin is followed by redemption; indeed, were it not for sin in the world, there would be no need for redemption. Man needs the purgation of pain and suffering. He needs to be reminded of his original sin in order to be saved.

Amy's way of life results in death: the death of her husband, her own death, and the death of her plans to manipulate time.

Eliot has Amy have three children in the play, Harry, Arthur, and John. They provide the Clytemnestra of his play with two additional sons to emphasize Amy's failure, for the two sons who have remained under her influence contrast sharply in awareness and intelligence with Harry. Also, their dullness allows the dramatist to relieve the tension of the scenes with moments of comedy. Arthur and John do not arrive on time to see their mother before her death because they have both met with automobile accidents on the way. Arthur's experience is typical. After running into (and demolishing) a roundsman's cart, he proceeds to back up into a shop window. Traveling at high speed at the time of the accident, he tells the policeman who had been chasing him, "I thought you were having a game with me." (92)

Atonement for sin is made by Harry alone, for he is Orestes, the heir to the family transgressions. Mary and Agatha play a passive role.[15] They have understood the predicament of Eliot's hero and are instrumental in his development. They function as intermediary characters, standing between Harry and the rest of the family. If not for them, Harry would have no one to confide in, for his uncles and aunts are insensitive to his suffering. Agatha and Mary are capable of talking effectively to the hero and aiding him in his development.

It is possible to analyze Harry's inability to communicate with his obtuse family in terms of Bergsonian thinking. According to Bergson, language reflects the orientation of the intellect towards practical ends and thus stereotypes experience into generalized, spatial symbols. Ordinary language can express only the awareness of time by individuals whose perceptions, like those of the family, are bounded by the conventionalized appearance of things.[16]

Because Eliot was deeply concerned with the simultaneous existence of a supernatural world alongside the natural one, he searched for methods of presenting the supernatural as a dramatic reality. His use of the Greek Furies is an attempt to reinterpret the ancient goddesses of dread as emissaries of God while still preserving, in the interests of his theme, that aspect which makes them most significant to the Greek story: their capacity to change. However, in reworking this element of the myth Eliot ran into difficulty. Commenting upon these figures years after the play was written, the dramatist is his harshest critic. In a consideration of the play's flaws, he notes:

> But the deepest flaw of all was in a failure of adjustment between the Greek story and the modern situation. I should either have stuck closer to Aeschylus or else taken a great deal more liberty with his myth. [And here apparently Eliot has the

*Oresteia* in mind, although he refers to Aeschylus' "myth."]
One evidence of this is the appearance of those ill-fated figures,
the Furies. They must, in future, be omitted from the cast,
and be understood to be visible only to certain of my characters
and not to the audience.[17]

The dramatist proceeds to describe the difficulties of presenting them on stage. Despite all efforts to make them "right" they
appeared like "uninvited guests" from a "fancy dress ball," a
"still out of a Walt Disney film" and even a "football team."
One suspects that such difficulties in presentation influenced
Eliot's entire view of these figures, especially when that view
came some ten years after the play was written. Difficulties do
exist in adjusting the Greek story to the modern situation because Eliot, unlike Jean-Paul Sartre, who handled the same
story for similar reasons, created a completely modern setting,
with modern characters firmly entrenched in their English
drawing room. Thus the appearance of the Eumenides seems
somewhat out of place, more so certainly than do the flies in
Sartre's Argos. O'Neill has created a modern setting, but his
Furies are all psychological.

Nevertheless, problems in presentation apart, the Eumenides do not weaken Eliot's play. This phase of the Greek story
adjusts easily to the modern situation when one realizes that
Eliot relied upon the religious significance of these Greek figures to develop his theme. They remain inhabitants of the
supernatural realm, but in the Christian context of the drama
they are "bright angels" rather than goddesses. In the transformation of the Greek Erinyes from goddesses of vengeance
to kindly deities Eliot saw an opportunity to present a visual
image of a changing attitude on the part of God and his agents
as they witness a corresponding change in Harry. Unlike the
ancient goddesses, Eliot's figures pursue his hero before the
death of his mother. They pursue him because he has already
sinned and incurred God's wrath by wishing for the death of
his wife. They first appear to him when he is talking to Mary.
Harry has yet to find his way; he is, at this point, grasping at
an imaginary life to escape his real one, and Mary realizes it.

She proposes the only solution to his problem: "What you need to alter is something inside you. (55) During this first encounter, they disapprove of Harry's actions, and they frighten him. Later, in the scene with Agatha, they produce an opposite effect. Harry addresses them:

> and this time
> You cannot think that I am surprised to see you.
> And you shall not think that I am afraid to see you.
> This time, you are real, this time, you are outside me. (106)

They are outside him because he has acknowledged them in acknowledging his sin. In desiring to atone for sin Harry is taking the first step towards receiving divine forgiveness. If the Eumenides frightened him previously, it was because their nature and their source were unknown to him and because he was being punished. His suffering, which was due to his lack of knowledge of God, ends when he comes to accept, and even pursue avidly, God's emissaries.

The predominant tone of the play is somber. It is true that Harry suffers no remorse for his mother's death, as did Orestes, but no one can doubt that he suffers. If one seeks to define the "emotion" of the play, it is surely Harry's anguish. Like the hero of Jean-Paul Sartre's *Les Mouches,* Harry suffers much more before the death of his mother than afterwards. This is due to the fact that both Eliot and Sartre view the murder itself as less important than the struggle of conscience which precedes it. The deed gains its significance from the fact that it is an expression of a new course of action, of a new life, in fact. All the pain has preceded the act. Harry's anguish results from his confusion of illusion and reality or, stated in terms of the time theme, from his ignorance of the true relationship between time and eternity. Until he becomes an enlightened man, he may accurately be described in Matthew Arnold's words, as "wandering between two worlds, one dead/The other powerless to be born."

In a famous declaration, T. S. Eliot had something explicit to say about emotion in drama:

> The only way of expressing emotion in the form of art is by
> finding an "objective correlative"; in other words, a set of ob-
> jects, a situation, a chain of events which shall be the formula
> of that *particular* emotion; such that when the external facts,
> which must terminate in sensory experience, are given, the
> emotion is immediately evoked.[18]

The external facts, or the situation, which are adequate — ideal,
in fact — to evoke Harry's emotion are contained in the mythological story. Orestes, too, wanders between two worlds. The
war between the deities has been none of his doing, yet it has
created an element of irrationality in the universe, which causes
Orestes' dilemma. At first glance, the story would appear to
hold little value for a monotheistic Christian seeking to explain
his faith. His rules of conduct are prescribed by an omnipotent,
omniscient God, whose justice is unquestionable. However
Eliot knew that the irrational element still persists in the world.
Earth is not quite a garden of Eden, though it was once. What
turned Eden into a "vale of tears" was what Eliot terms "Adam's
curse." The surface events of the myth: the family curse, the
hero's exile and return, his act against his mother, and his
eventual rehabilitation provide the "scaffolding" Eliot was discussing in his essay on Joyce's *Ulysses*. They allow the artist to
develop his hero as he portrays him reacting to a view of reality
advanced by the family to which he returns.

To bring out his themes, Eliot must go beneath the surface,
but he needs that surface to function as a starting point. There
must be an interplay between external and internal meaning;
one must give rise inevitably to the other. Thus the event of
Orestes returning from physical exile to the land of his origins
suggests and parallels the experience of a man returning from
spiritual exile to a reunion with his Creator. *The Family Reunion* is, undoubtedly, the product of a man who was a classicist
in literature and an Anglo-Catholic in religion.

Four years after Eliot tried his hand at renovating the
Orestes myth, Jean-Paul Sartre became interested in the same
tale for similar reasons. Like Eliot, the French dramatist re-

jected what he regarded as a narrow and abstract view, the perspective of psychology. He believed that the emotion of a tale, such as "the fascism of Creon, the stubbornness of Antigone" must be considered against a background of religious and moral values, social demands, and social and political conflicts.[19] Employing a method close to that of the author of *The Family Reunion*, he placed the protagonist of *Les Mouches* (1943) within a set of circumstances and demonstrated his reaction to events as exemplary of a type. Just as the conflicts between the characters of Eliot's play result from opposing views of life, those between the figures in *Les Mouches* spring from discordant ethical positions. Sartre, too, seizes on and attaches new meanings to the terms "exile" and "reconciliation." The action of the original tale is seen once more as a spiritual experience. The difference is that the actions of the hero of the French drama involve a negation of Christianity. Sartre turned to classical mythology for his material in order to create a work that would illustrate his existentialist creed.

One objection to Sartre's use of mythological material was made by Francis Fergusson, who feels that it is pointless for the dramatist to reach back into antiquity for inspiration. Contemporary life, he argues, offers many examples of extreme situations, such as a visit to the dentist, which strikes him as "an inescapable ordeal with an obsessive power; a form of torment which threatens the very basis of human freedom and which only the heroic can survive with dignity." [20] However the situation that interests the existentialist must be one offering the individual an opportunity to make significant choices which will so determine his acts as to change his entire life and even influence the life of the community of which he is a part. Sartre would agree that one is constantly choosing, but the decision concerning the trip to the dentist has as much significance, the French author would say, as the choice one is sometimes called upon to make between a cream puff and a chocolate eclair. The point is that the choice must be accompanied by a struggle of consciousness, by an anguish. Myths project an image of this struggle. The Orestes myth recounts the dilemma of a man whose actions are divinely ordained and divinely vetoed. Clearly, his freedom is obstructed, and he suffers thereby. In its fundamentally religious meaning, the myth explores man's relationship with supernatural forces and considers the problems resulting from his existence in the world. It seeks to illuminate the meaning of human life. Ultimately, the myth aims at an existential meaning. What Jean-Paul Sartre has done in *Les Mouches* is to explore one of the many possibilities for action open to a man in Orestes' position.

The French dramatist, like Eliot, made use of various devices to bring the drama close to contemporary experience. Eliot's setting may appear to be more modern, for his drama occurs in a manor house in twentieth-century England rather than in the palace of ancient Argos, where Sartre's hero plays out his role; despite the fact that Eliot's characters speak poetry, often ambiguous at times, they do go to birthday parties, drive fast automobiles, and read current events in the daily newspapers. *Les Mouches*, however, has its share of modernisms, more striking, perhaps, than those of *The Family Reunion*, for they stand out against their ancient setting. Sartre's innovations include characters who speak colloquial prose, such as the guards in the palace whom we hear in conversation. Defining themselves as "roturiers," or ordinary folk, they remind us of the soldiers in *La Machine infernale*. Their chief concern is inspection by their superiors, and the townsfolk of Argos, like the townspeople of *Mourning Becomes Electra*, are given a modern social reality by their indulgence in gossip.

However, characters and locale retain their Greek names in *Les Mouches*, and the unities are preserved. Sartre's method is to respect the traditional plot (more so than Eliot), for it is through that plot that the French dramatist can express his own meanings. The modern Orestes returns home, is reunited with Electra, and literally and brutally murders Clytemnestra and Aegisthus.

Commenting on simplicity in plot and character development, Sartre reveals that his model is classic tragedy:

. . . if one approaches politics or love by slow degrees, then
acute problems, arising suddenly, call for no progression. By
taking our dramatic personae and precipitating them, in the
very first scene, into the highest pitch of their conflicts we
turn to the well-known pattern of classic tragedy, which always
seizes upon the action at the very moment it is headed for
catastrophe.[21]

Oreste's homecoming initiates the action of *Les Mouches*. The
taut structure that Sartre imposes on his material does not
hamper him from introducing and highlighting meanings
which, taken together, make his version of the tragedy a
decidedly individual achievement. It is true that Orestes returns home, confronts the sister who has long dreamed of his
return and his vengeance, and is precipitated immediately into
conflict. One element is missing, however. Sartre seeks no
parallel to a deterministic view of life in the Greek tragedy.
He writes a play about a totally free man. Thus, in order to
transform the tragedy of fatality into a drama of choice, the
modern dramatist eliminates the fatality. He begins by eliminating the oracle. Unlike the Greek hero who has, upon his
arrival in Argos, already accepted the dictates of Apollo, Sartre's
Oreste comes to town as a tourist. What the modern dramatist
has discarded with the oracle is the divine hand guiding the
events. Oreste no longer concerns himself with a god's commands. If his detachment is possible because the oracle does
not exist, it is also explainable by a Sartrean addition: the hero
of the modern play moves outside the circle of the god's influence because he has been acquiring lessons in Stoic and Epi-
curean philosophy from his companion-tutor, a Pylades who
denies the existence of Apollo.[22] Even though Oreste is under
no divine compulsion to return home, his sense of rootlessness,
of the lack of direction of his life — a pressure perhaps as strong
as the oracular one — leads him to desert the smooth road of
the tourist and turn towards the land of his origin.

Prior to his arrival in the city, Oreste's movements had

been aimless. The kind of freedom he had enjoyed — and his tutor boasts of it — lacked responsibility. His life had been distinguished by no significant deeds. Even the relatively insignificant adventures of childhood, adventures which would have made the man, were not part of his experience. Oreste has spent laborious days following his tutor's advice that he prepare himself for a chair in philosophy or architecture in a great university, and as he gazes at the palace door through which he might have passed while on any number of escapades, he comments authoritatively, "That's the Dorian style, isn't it? What do you think of that gold inlay? I saw something similar at Dodona: it's beautiful work." [23]

Sartre provides Oreste with a background of uncommitted activity in order to prepare him for a present in which the possibility to choose involvement can exist. If that keen sense of the inevitable working out of a curse is absent from *Les Mouches*, it is in large part due to the fact that the past has no influence upon future events. To the existentialist there is no such thing as cosmic time. The important time is the present, for this is the time of anxiety and choice. The future is simply the time of unlimited possibility. Unlike T. S. Eliot's hero who searches the past for the man he might have been, Sartre's hero looks forward to a new, free life in the future. The image in Oreste's mind is not of a Jamesian specter; it is of a couple who wait in expectation and in hope. When he pleads with Electra not to heed Jupiter but to follow him, he must admit that he is not sure where he is going. Nevertheless, he assures his sister that "beyond the rivers and the mountains are an Oreste and an Electre who wait for us." (185)

Where dramatists like O'Neill and Eliot have tried to find some modern equivalent for the ancestral transgression, which calls down the wrath of the gods upon the house of Atreus and predisposes future generations to crime, Sartre concentrates on developing a plausible present, a protagonist in a state of being that, in existentialist terms, is equivalent to that existence which precedes the hero's assertion of self. Of course, in doing away with the curse (or some potent equivalent), the dramatist loses much of the power of the original story. The suspense evoked by the unravelling of a fearful past is necessarily absent. There are no opportunities for Ibsen-like revelations of gory ghosts in the palatial closets. Sartre can create no character like Agatha or Cassandra (or even a minor figure such as Seth, the watchman of O'Neill's Mannons) to strike a note of impending gloom. There is a substitute of sorts. We watch the protagonist move through the inevitable progress of the existentialist from awareness through choice through act. Foreshadowing consists mainly of forecasting the next stage in Oreste's development.

Although Apollo's influence is absent, the presence of the king of the Olympian gods is very much felt in *Les Mouches*. Throughout much of the play Jupiter can be seen stalking Oreste through the streets of Argos in an effort to persuade the young prince to leave town. However, Sartre's hero does not heed the words of the god, whose influence is confined to those who have not made the most important discovery of their lives, that of the absolute nature of their freedom. As Oreste overhears Jupiter tell Egisthe, "Once freedom pierces a man's soul, the gods are powerless against him." (157) Jupiter is aware that Oreste represents a danger to the power of the gods because the young man comes to know that — once his existence has been determined — the laws of the gods cannot restrain his actions. The confrontation between Oreste and Jupiter is essentially a confrontation between the god in his role as traditional dispenser of justice — and it is in this capacity that he serves Sartre's purposes — and the man who proclaims, "Justice is a matter between men, and I do not need a God to teach it to me." (159) The justice that Sartre's Jupiter has been distributing in Argos has been determined according to the nature of the crime or, perversely, by the degree to which the offender's crime has pleased the king of the gods. The criteria for pleasing Jupiter, and thus avoiding celestial wrath and condemnation, are the amount of guilt and remorse the individual assumes and the degree to which he is willing to subordinate his liberty and devote himself to acts of atonement. Divine forgiveness follows self-enslavement. Such a realization helps to release Oreste from the confines of his situation, that is from those moral, religious, political, and social barriers that delineate his society, "from the limits which enclose him on all sides." [24] (Of course, "situation" for Sartre implies much more than the total of those conditions to which we generally give the name "environment." Man's situation is his relationship with those objective forces that he organizes and gives meaning to by his goals. Situations vary as man alters this relationship, but what is constant is the necessity for choice within the situation.) The farther he moves from his situation, the farther he moves from the world of nature — a fact that becomes apparent in that very theatrical scene (curiously reminiscent of Satan's temptation of Christ) in which Jupiter shows Oreste the breadth of his powers and urges him to rejoin the universe. It is to a universe of stony objects that the god would have him reconcile himself.

By transferring the domain of justice from Olympus to Earth, Sartre reduces the myth to human — and even humanistic — terms. Oreste's protests, which affirm, in effect, that man has greater dignity than rocks and stones, proclaim a basic tenet of Sartre's existentialism. The French philosopher is very careful to define his concept of humanism. Man exists in a human universe, the universe of human subjectivity. By projecting himself outside of himself and by pursuing transcendent goals, man is able to fulfill himself. As he seeks to do so he is cognizant of the fact that he is the sole legislator.[25] Much of Sartre's thinking on this matter is rather abstract and difficult to translate into dramatic terms. He is aided, though, by the mythological material, which raises questions about the nature of justice and human behavior. However, the myth ends by relating that human justice is faulty. The twelve citizens who constitute the jury cannot legislate. A divine hand must intervene. Sartre transforms the myth so that his Oreste becomes jury and judge. Such is the significance of his proclamation that justice is a matter between men.

Existentialist subjectivity is based on the principle: "Man equals the sum total of his acts." [26] Sartre's philosophy is one that places the emphasis on doing, on the importance of the act. Reality equals action, and a man is alive to the extent that he realizes himself in action. (On the basis of such a belief, Sartre maintains that when we criticize him on the grounds that his thinking is pessimistic, we actually are taking notice of a firm optimism.[27]) Oreste's discovery of his freedom is insufficient to allow him to define himself. He must affirm his belief with an act that will be the outward expression of the kind of man he has chosen to be. Thus, not any act will do. It must be the act of an individual who has realized that he has an identity apart from that of a natural object; it must be an act that will enable him to transcend the limits of his situation. In Sartre's version of the tale, the act is the matricide. The murder that Oreste commits is real, and it is necessary that it be real. Oreste does not drive his mother to suicide because Sartre, unlike Eugene O'Neill, discounts psychological motives.[28] The French dramatist is not, like T. S. Eliot, concerned merely with the intent to commit crime because he discounts Christian thinking on sin. The act remains as it was in the original myth — real, bloody, and horrific.

Sartre changes only the motive. Following the events and the literal meaning of the myth, the French dramatist presents his hero with an opportunity to choose vengeance. Indeed, all the other characters view the murder as something more than a possibility, and all are aware of Oreste's duty to avenge Agamemnon. The circumstances provide for such an act. What is unexpected, what is very new in Oreste's behavior, is his reason for acting. He murders to validate his freedom. Were vengeance his motive one would have to question, as does Maurice Cranston, the extent to which Sartre can uphold the rightness of such a feudal ethos.[29] The point is that his hero does not murder for vengeance. Vengeance, followed by remorse, remains an important aspect of the drama; it is not discarded. However, it functions to provide the hero with an alternative, with a chance to negate his newly-discovered independence. Were Oreste to murder in the name of vengeance, his act would enslave him further.

Alternate ways to live life are presented to the hero of

*Les Mouches* mainly in the example of the other characters. When the tottering Egisthe looks up at the man who has dealt him a mortal blow and gasps out, as he breathes his last, "Is it true that you feel no remorse?" (158) we are tempted to scold Sartre for his poor dramaturgy. The comment, coming when it does, appears to be ludicrous. What saves the moment (and the play) is the fact that we are not watching simply a confrontation between a murderer and his victim. The conflict between the two is essentially that between different ways of life.[30] Sartre's philosophical writings abound with examples of "inauthentic" types as he seeks to differentiate modes of behavior among men. The individual lives in society, and he is necessarily involved with others. Frequently the relations with others may involve conflict. Instead of narrating experiences of encounters with "inauthentic" individuals, as he does in his essays, Sartre dramatizes such encounters in *Les Mouches*. In each scene he places his hero — the exemplar of his personal ethical position — against a practitioner of opposing views. Sartre makes use of conflicts between the characters in the Greek story to create clashes between his modern characters and the essences they represent. Because we expect the conflict we can concentrate on the new motives with which the existentialist author furnishes his characters. Thus we know that Aegisthus and Orestes are traditional enemies. The conflict remains, for certainly it is one of the crucial elements in the surface story, but the antagonism becomes more complex. It depends now upon opposing value systems. As we have noted previously, T. S. Eliot does much the same thing in *The Family Reunion* for identical reasons; the main difference in Eliot's treatment involves the nature of the position his characters assume.

An exception and a surprise is the conflict between Oreste and Electre, for traditionally they have had their great cause in common. Their separation causes the protagonist grief in the midst of his triumph and makes his resolution to pursue his own course even more heroic. When we first meet Electre, she is the devoted sister who eagerly awaits the return of her

brother. She hates her mother and scorns the sovereignty of
Egisthe. Her refusal to give her assent to the status quo in
Argos has resulted in her social disgrace, and she thinks only
of the brother who will one day arrive to destroy her oppressors.

Electre is useful to Sartre because she points to a course
of action open to his hero. She is, in many ways, like her
brother. She is in conflict with the rulers of Argos, and she
realizes that the people are being deceived. She, too, is free of
superstition and admonishes the crowd of Argives, "What
are you afraid of? I look all around you and I see only
your shadows." (126) Not only does Electre try to enlighten
the people with her words, she attempts to demonstrate her
fearlessness by her actions, which accounts for her dancing.
Despite the sign from Jupiter that interrupts her dance, she
insists, "So? I missed the mark this time. Next time I'll do
better." (129) Interestingly enough, it is Electre who first
presents to Oreste the possibility of choice:

> Suppose qu'un gars de Corinthe, un de ces gars qui rient le
> soir avec les filles, trouve, au retour d'un voyage, son père
> assassiné, sa mère dans le lit du meurtrier et sa sœur en escla-
> vage, est-ce qu'il filerait doux, le gars de Corinthe, est-ce qu'il
> s'en irait à reculons, en faisant des révérences, chercher des
> consolations auprès de ses amies? ou bien est-ce qu'il sortirait
> son épée et est-ce qu'il cognerait sur l'assassin jusqu'à lui faire
> éclater la tête?

> Suppose some young fellow from Corinth, one who laughs
> with girls in the evenings, were to find, upon returning home
> from a trip, his father assassinated, his mother living with his
> murderer, and his sister treated as a slave, would he just shirk
> his responsibility, begging everyone's pardon, and run to his
> friends for consolation? Or would he draw his sword, pounce
> upon the assassin and split open his head? (105)

However, the choice Electre offers her brother is between
total withdrawal or commitment in the name of vengeance.
The Oreste of her imagination rages in his passion; his head is

lowered and he mutters angry words. There is a part of Electre's nature which creates a breach between herself and her brother. Her dream of happiness is not involvement; it is of boys and girls walking together freely, as in Corinth. She understands nothing of Oreste's desire to belong to Argos; she can speak only of "happy towns." The significant result of Sartre's recognition scene is that the brother and sister fail to find some common ground on which to base their future activity. Two opposing points of view confront each other. Electre dreams only of vengeance; she cannot see beyond being released from her present misery. So far apart are they that Electre continues to call her brother "Philèbe" after he has identified himself. The attempts the Argive princess has made to contact her people have proved feeble. Her judgment is that only violence can accomplish something, for her words have not been heard. She tells Oreste:

> J'ai voulu croire que je pourrais guérir les gens d'ici par des paroles. Tu as vu ce qui est arrivé: ils aiment leur mal, ils ont besoin d'une plaie familière qu'ils entretiennent soigneusement en la grattant de leurs ongles sales. C'est par la violence qu'il faut les guérir, car on ne peut vaincre le mal que par un autre mal.

> I wanted to believe that I could cure these people with words. You saw what happened. They nurse their ills; they must like their sores, for they aggravate them by scratching them with dirty finger nails. It's only through violence that they can be cured, since evil is only conquered by evil. (132)

Although she argues for violence, she balks at it. Her inability to commit herself to any course of action — not even to the one she advocates — extends even to a reluctance to see the dreams that have sustained her come true. As she stands over the body of Egisthe in anticipation of Clytemnestre's screams, she is puzzled by her reaction and wonders if she has been lying to herself during the past fifteen years. Electre is guilty of a self-deception that constitutes "bad faith" for Sartre. Her unwillingness consciously to assume her freedom and involve herself in action marks her life as being, in the terminology of the existentialist, "inauthentic." Electre may be a failure as an existentialist heroine; however, the crime of passion she urges is consistent with her impulsive, passionate nature. There are moments when she exhibits great excitement in sharp contrast to the more controlled Oreste.

Electre's existence is not the only one that is inauthentic. In this regard, she moves close to the citizens of Argos themselves who, like Oreste, have had the opportunity to express their freedom but who have remained, instead, uncommitted and dormant under the burden of remorse which Agamemnon's murder has imposed on his city. All the townspeople wear mourning, but the crime they atone for is not their own. They are not even willing to accept responsibility for their own private peccadilloes. Along with Clytemnestre, they view public confession as a sort of game, a national pastime. In this last respect, they take their cue from Egisthe, who publicly acknowledges that Agamemnon is the man whom he has killed with his own hands.

Egisthe has been making that admission for the past fifteen years. The crime he acknowledges so glibly has no value, however. In order to bring out his own meanings, the dramatist creates a contrast between the crime Egisthe committed and that of Oreste. Egisthe's murder of Agamemnon was not an act of defiance, or self-assertion. Jupiter characterizes it as a clumsy crime, one which "did not know itself." (154) In contrast, Oreste's crime is a defiant, remorseless act which, insofar as it is a free expression of a free man, rivals an act of the god's. Egisthe has no need of Jupiter's pronouncements. He has recognized his own failing, as he readily admits, "I come, I go, I cry out in loud tones, I parade my frowning countenance, and those who see me cringe in repentance. But I am only an empty shell." (149) He is what Oreste would have become had the young man shied away from killing him. In similar language Oreste, prior to his deed, describes himself: "I am barely living: I am the most ghostly of all the ghosts who haunt this town today." (136)

The life of Egisthe is nothing more than the image he has built of himself. "What am I, except the fear that others have of me?" (156) he asks. Although all his acts have been aimed at creating an image of dread, he shudders at it. Egisthe shares with Jupiter the knowledge that is the bane of gods and kings. He knows that men are free. He admits to Clytemnestre, "For fifteen years I have been playing the part of a scarecrow." (148) Egisthe has been masquerading. He is, like his Greek ancestor, a usurper, a false king. His illegitimacy is seen, in existentialist terms, as inauthenticity. He has failed to lead a life of commitment and, in addition, he has conspired to prevent others from doing likewise.

Sartre, of course, would quickly add that the people themselves are in bad faith if they plead the excuse of tyranny. However, insofar as Egisthe is a tyrant, he is guilty of deception on two counts: the deceit he has practiced on the Argives by not revealing to them the secret of their freedom is merely a reflection of his self-deception. Presumably, a king who has the welfare of his people at heart would act as Oreste does. Egisthe's political significance remains. He has usurped Oreste's place, and when the young prince murders him, Oreste receives, as his patrimony, the city. The sole act of Sartre's hero as king is to restore to the Argives their freedom.

On the thematic level, Sartre grasped the same aspect of the myth that T. S. Eliot reworked in *The Family Reunion*. If the Greek Orestes moves from alienation to reconciliation, Sartre's Oreste may be said to have a similar experience, though alienation and reconciliation take on new meanings for the French dramatist. On the literal level, the hero of *Les Mouches*, like his Greek counterpart, experiences a physical exile that is real enough. The years between his expulsion from and return to his native Argos have been spent wandering through foreign cities and among strange landmarks.

The physical exile exists alongside a more acute, spiritual exile. Describing his activities Oreste discloses, "I go from town to town, a stranger to others and to myself." (136) Oreste is conscious of a void within himself: a void caused by the fact that, although he can remember that of the three hundred and eighty-seven steps of the temple of Ephesus, the seventeenth is broken, he has none of the memories he might have possessed had he remained at home "for memories are luxuries reserved for those who possess homes, animals, servants, and land." (96) Unlike T. S. Eliot's Harry, he has no ties, familial or otherwise, and unlike the hero of *The Family Reunion*, he cannot even look forward to recapturing something of the essence of his childhood as a first step towards reintegrating himself.[31]

When Oreste listens patiently to his tutor's tirade on the absence of hospitality in Argos and counters with the simple announcement, "I was born here," (82) he puts an end to his physical exile. However, in order to terminate his exile from self he must first become converted to the philosophy of involvement; he must seek his identity as an individual. The act of murder that he commits, as we have seen, accomplished such a goal. Further, it allows him to assume his proper place among the men of his city by giving him the opportunity to burden himself with all the crimes and remorse of Argos. The murder allows him to manifest his social consciousness. It has been argued that the murder does little to relate Oreste to the Argives and that a great distance remains to separate Sartre's hero from his people.[32] However, one must always bear in mind that Sartre has followed the surface events of the myth. With the death of Egisthe and Clytemnestre, Oreste is restored his lost patrimony; and in evaluating Oreste's position vis-à-vis the Argives, one must keep in mind the literal meaning of the myth. As a result of his act Oreste has become king. He has been keenly aware of his aristocratic heritage throughout the drama. Despite some early protests to the contrary, his deep regret has been that:

> Je n'ai pas vu naître un seul de leurs enfants, ni assisté aux noces de leurs filles, je ne partage pas leurs remords et je ne connais pas un seul de leurs noms. C'est le barbu qui a raison: un roi doit avoir les mêmes souvenirs que ses sujets.

I have not seen one of their children come into the world, nor
been present at the marriage of their daughters; I do not share
their remorse, I do not know one of them by name. That
bearded fellow is right: a king should have the same memories
as his subjects. (97)

His act enables him to share the remorse of his subjects at
the same time that it permits him to assume a social position by
virtue of which he exerts an influence as powerful as that which
enabled Egisthe to enslave his people. The relationship of
Oreste to the Argives has been altered as a result of his act. He
has drawn closer to them in a number of ways, and when he
says, "I wish to be a king without land and without subjects,"
he means that he will give up the throne because he seeks
dominion over himself alone, for to rule others is inevitably to
deny them their freedom. It is paradoxical, but Oreste's contact with his people is strongest when he leaves them. In
taking on their remorse and granting them freedom he performs
an act of supreme love. Indeed, Hazel E. Barnes feels that by
taking away the Furies, Oreste is performing an act that is
equivalent to the divine one. His suffering for mankind is
Christ-like.[33] Furthermore, because Oreste has inherited the
throne of Argos, and because only he has the opportunity only
he can perform such a sacrifice. Although he was born a prince
of the Argives, his exile made him a citizen of another city,
Corinth. The fact that the murder reestablishes the validity of
the social position he held at birth is one reason why he tells
Electre, immediately after the murder, "I feel as if I have given
you life and I have just been born with you." (162)

Oreste, unlike the Greek hero, is totally free of remorse
and fear of the gods. Although the Furies, identified with the
flies of the title, are quite real and inflict physical punishment,
Oreste tolerates them because he has voluntarily offered himself to them. Oreste has no fear because he can tell Jupiter with
conviction that he is not the king of men. However, there is a
moment in Oreste's experience which, in certain respects, parallels the remorse of the Greek hero. Insofar as the dramatist
concerns himself with personal suffering as he handles the

mythological material, Sartre has used this element to good advantage, for it forms an inseparable part of the experience involved in the making of an existentialist. The Greek figure suffers when he comes to feel the full significance of his act, and Oreste, similarly, comes to know pain when he realizes what his act entails.

At the moment that Oreste realizes that he is free and that he is the possessor of what Sartre terms, "the total responsibility of his existence"[34] and, in fact, the responsibility of all men, he experiences a feeling of anguish accompanied by a sense of forlornness. The feeling becomes greater the more he becomes cognizant of the fact that when he chooses, and his choice is made for all men, he simultaneously affirms the value of that choice. What bothers him is the knowledge that his task — that of creating his essence — is essentially a lonely one, for no idea of God, no *a priori* system of ethics exists for him. Oreste describes his experience to Jupiter:

> Tout à coup, la liberté a fondu sur moi et m'a transi, la nature a sauté en arrière, et je n'ai plus eu d'âge, et je me suis senti tout seul, au milieu de ton petit monde bénin, comme quelqu'un qui a perdu son ombre; et il n'y a plus rien eu au ciel, ni Bien ni Mal, ni personne pour me donner des ordres.

> Suddenly, liberty struck me and benumbed me; nature sprang back, and the years of my youth were gone. I felt myself all alone, in the midst of your mild little world, like someone who has lost his shadow; and there was nothing left in heaven, no good or evil, nor anyone to give me orders. (182)

Oreste's act causes him pain because it isolates him from the world in which he has previously lived, much the way that the act of the Greek prince singles him out among men as a transgressor of sacred law. Jupiter tells Sartre's hero, "Your liberty is only an infection that consumes you while it isolates you; it is only an exile." (182) Oreste replies, "Yes, it is an exile." However, the exile that Oreste is faced with at this point is something he has come to expect. It has been noted that when the existentialist negates the old collective ("essences" and so on), the resulting homelessness and estrangement is something that he has come to expect and even look upon as a final "resting" point.[35] Oreste knows that exile from the world of nature means reconciliation with his true self. The isolation of which Jupiter speaks differs radically from that sense of rootlessness that had disturbed him prior to the murder. It is an isolation that enables him to commit himself to a course of action. Although few follow his example — not even Electre follows him — he goes into a voluntary exile. It is only in such isolation that by taking on the burden of the Furies he can contribute to the welfare of others.

That aspect of the myth that involved the experience of exile intrigued both Sartre and T. S. Eliot. Their concern with the theme was due to the fact that their dramas centered around a moment of perception. Each author wanted to show his hero being converted to a view of existence he himself shared, and such conversion is most effective when the individual is involved in that spiritual exile that signifies the absence of belief. The discovery of the hero is the discovery of a set of values that leads him to freedom. The philosophical position that each hero assumes differs (to be expected in view of the fact that among contemporary philosophers no wide philosophical agreement is in evidence). What is most interesting is that each author interprets the identical story to produce a view of life that is totally different from the other. Jean-Paul Sartre, reworking various elements of the myth, produces an Orestes who is an atheistic existentialist, and T. S. Eliot, doing much the same thing, produces an Orestes who is a Christian. Both heroes, involved in a situation requiring immediate and significant choice, gain awareness of their plight and arrive at an ethical position to which they remain passionately committed.

The search for self-definition in both plays is successful, and we can easily visualize Oreste and Harry walking off in the sunset, their eyes fixed confidently on the horizon. However, the struggle has taken its toll. The hero remains alive, it is true, and few corpses are strewn on the stage, and at least one hero,

Harry, has the promise of eternal life. Nevertheless, death has occurred, not only the physical deaths of Clytemnestre or Amy, but the kind of death that occurs more frequently in everyday life. Eric Bentley, speaking of such death, comments:

> We see ourselves as experiencing little deaths all the time. Lying down to sleep is a little death. Saying good-bye is a little death. In both cases, a piece of life is surrendered, and to give anything up is always to die.[36]

What Mr. Bentley has in mind is the kind of death that Mary experiences when Harry rejects her. Describing the end of her hopes, she creates one of the saddest moments in the play:

> Of course it was much too late
> Then for anything to come for me: I should have known it;
> It was all over, I believe, before it began;
> But I deceived myself. It takes so many years
> To learn that one is dead! [37]

Similarly, there is poignancy in the parting of Sartre's Oreste from Electre, especially because the affection he has demonstrated for her has been genuine.

*The Family Reunion* and *Les Mouches* are both austere dramas. The French drama is particularly so because it lacks the poetry of Eliot's play. The unities are preserved in each case, and only one event occupies the dramatist: the experience of his hero. If the hero is a "type" character it is because the dramatist wishes to give the impression that the hero's fate is a common one. Discussing his problem, Harry states the case well:

> But it begins to seem just part of some huge disaster,
> Some monstrous mistake and aberration
> Of all men, of the world, which I cannot put in order.[38]

Both authors are of a philosophical bent. And the soul of the plays they write is in the thematic statement.

## ※ NOTES

[1] T. S. Eliot, *The Family Reunion* (New York: Harcourt, Brace & World, Inc.), p. 31. All subsequent page references to this edition will be given immediately after the quotation.

[2] John Peter, "The Family Reunion," *Scrutiny*, XVI (1949), p. 220.

[3] T. S. Eliot, *Four Quartets* (New York: Harcourt, Brace & World, Inc., 1943), p. 3.

[4] Georges Poulet, *Studies in Human Time*, trans. Elliott Coleman (Baltimore: The Johns Hopkins Press, 1956), p. 356.

[5] Maud Bodkin, *The Quest for Salvation in an Ancient and a Modern Play* (London: Oxford University Press, 1941), p. 46.

[6] D. W. Harding, "Progression of Theme in Eliot's Modern Plays," *The Kenyon Review*, Vol. XVIII, No. 3 (Summer, 1956), p. 342.

[7] The psychoanalytic interpretation is most thoroughly worked out by C. L. Barber in "Strange Gods at T. S. Eliot's *The Family Reunion*" in *T. S. Eliot: A Selected Critique*, ed. Leonard Unger (New York: Holt, Rinehart & Winston, Inc., 1948), pp. 415–43. Barber feels that the play's meaning is unintelligible unless certain ambiguities are resolved by such interpretation. He sees the action of the play as a "vehicle for hostile impulses toward wife and mother and towards the world in general as represented by the family." (430) Harry is the neurotic seeking the security of perfect love.

[8] Leonard Unger, *The Man in the Name: Essays on the Experience of Poetry* (Minneapolis: The University of Minnesota Press, 1956), p. 182.

[9] Another Heraclitean observation.

[10] Philip Wheelwright, in *Heraclitus* (Princeton: Princeton University Press, 1959), p. 100, observes that in spatial representation the truth of the idea that the beginning and the end are common is manifested in the geometrical figure of the circle.

[11] T. S. Eliot, "Vergil and the Christian World," *Sewanee Review*, LXI (1953), p. 10.

[12] Carol H. Smith, *T. S. Eliot's Dramatic Theory and Practice* (Princeton: Princeton University Press, 1963), p. 134.

[13] Eliot's belief that "the beginning and the end are common" is, of course, basic to his entire philosophy. The theme is fully explored in "East Coker," which was written during the same period as *The Family Reunion*. The title of the poem is the name of a village in Somersetshire which was the birthplace of philosopher Sir Thomas Elyot. It was from this village by the sea that ancestor Andrew Eliot set out for America in the seventeenth century. At the time of T. S. Eliot's death, newspaper accounts revealed that the poet's last wish had been fulfilled: his ashes were placed in the church at East Coker.

[14] Eliot, *Four Quartets, op. cit.*, p. 22.

[15] Agatha explains to Mary that they are "only watchers and waiters." (49) Her words have a Miltonic ring and one recalls the image of the seventeenth-century poet lamenting the passing of his days. As he developed his views on time, Eliot must certainly have had Milton in mind. The essence of the modern poet's thinking is summed up in the sonnet "On Time" in which the Christian Milton advises a gluttonous Time to run out its race, for it will consume itself and then Eternity will bring man to the foot of the "supreme Throne," where he will remain forever, "Triumphing over Death, and Chance, and thee/O Time."

[16] See Anne Ward, "Speculations on Eliot's Time-World: An analysis of *The Family Reunion* in relation to Hulme and Bergson," *American Literature*, XXI (1949), p. 28.

[17] T. S. Eliot, "The Family Reunion" in *Playwrights on Playwriting*, ed. Toby Cole (New York: Hill & Wang, Inc., 1960), p. 256.

[18] T. S. Eliot, *Selected Essays* (New York: Harcourt, Brace & World, Inc., 1950), pp. 124–25.

[19] Jean-Paul Sartre, "Forgers of Myth: the Young Playwrights of France," *Theatre Arts*, XXX (June, 1946), p. 326.

[20] Francis Fergusson, "Sartre as Playwright," *Partisan Review*, XVI (April, 1949), p. 410.

[21] Sartre, "Forgers of Myth," p. 331.

[22] Oreste has surpassed his tutor in one respect, as Theophil Spoerri has pointed out in "The Structure of Existence: *The Flies*," *Sartre: A Collection of Critical Essays*, ed. Edith Kern (Englewood Cliffs: Prentice-Hall, Inc. 1962), p. 56. The tutor is "spiritually false and metaphysically blind," whereas Oreste possesses a feeling for the presence of Jupiter. Aside from being the opposite of the Pylades of the *Choephoroe*, who prods Orestes to action, Sartre's figure also represents the contemptible intellectual who spends his days reading and talking, but never acting.

[23] Jean-Paul Sartre, *Huis Clos; Les Mouches* (Paris: Gallimard, 1947), p. 96. Subsequent page references to this edition will be given immediately after the quotation.

[24] Sartre, "Forgers of Myth," p. 325.

[25] Jean-Paul Sartre, *L'Existentialisme est un humanisme* (Paris: Nagel, 1946), pp. 92–4.

[26] *Ibid.*, p. 22.

[27] *Ibid.*, p. 58.

[28] So little time is spent developing the character of Clytemnestra in *Les Mouches* that she is hardly realized. Her greatest usefulness results from the fact that she is available to be murdered.

[29] Maurice Cranston, *Sartre* (London: Oliver & Boyd, Ltd., 1962), p. 37.

[30] In view of the fact that *Les Mouches* made its appearance in 1943, a popular interpretation sees the drama as a political parallel to events in France during World War II. The conflict between Oreste and Jupiter, for example, is seen as one between the prince as a symbol of the Resistance movement who stands against an oppressive Jupiter, seen as representing the Nazi occupation. See, for example, Hazel E. Barnes, *The Literature of Possibility* (Lincoln: University of Nebraska Press, 1959), p. 95. Viewed in this way, the play resembles another French drama, produced under similar circumstances and (if one follows similar critical lines) utilizing the myth to suggest political parallels, namely Jean Anouilh's *Antigone*.

[31] Thinking of his childhood, Oreste can only recall, "I knew at the age of seven that I was an exile. . . ." (95)

[32] Francis Jeanson, *Sartre par lui-même* (Paris: Aux Editions du Seuil, 1955), p. 25.

[33] Barnes, *op. cit.*, p. 94.

[34] Sartre, *L'Existentialisme est un humanisme*, p. 24.

[35] Harry Slochower, "The Function of Myth in Existentialism," *Yale French Studies*, I, No. 1, p. 43.

[36] Eric Bentley, *The Life of the Drama* (New York: Atheneum Publishers, 1964), p. 273.

[37] T. S. Eliot, *The Family Reunion*, p. 117.

[38] *Ibid.*, p. 88.

# ❊ III

## ❊ The Modern Rebel

Had Henry de Montherlant so wished he, too, could have extracted a profound religious significance from the substance of a myth. The opportunity was present in the tale of Pasiphaé, the legendary queen of Crete. The ancient story tells of a clash between Minos, husband of Pasiphaé and king of Crete, and Poseidon, god of the sea. The subject of the quarrel is a magnificent white bull, sent by Poseidon to Minos in answer to the latter's prayer for proof of his favor with the gods. Human transgression occurs when Minos, beside himself with admiration for the beautiful animal, attempts to deceive the god by returning an inferior bull in its place. Divine retribution follows: Poseidon inspires Pasiphaé with a passion for the creature that far exceeds that of her husband's. Montherlant, intrigued with the idea of interpreting the myth in dramatic terms while focusing upon the episode involving Pasiphaé, is aware of the possibility of developing a religious theme. A hypothetical Pasiphaé could be viewed as a sort of queen-priestess-goddess, whose most significant action — sexual commerce with a bull — is meant to represent contact with a divine force culminating in religious ecstasy. However, the French writer failed to find sufficient dramatic interest in such an approach: "Pasiphaé offering herself to the bull in the spirit of a religious being who is about to receive a sacrament is not material to interest a writer of tragedies."

Another hypothesis is possible. The episode involving Pasiphaé and the bull can be abstracted so that the mythological situation reduces itself to the following: "A human being finds himself on the verge of an act which the code of his society rejects and which he desires to commit. He decides to commit it." [1] Mindful of his poet's right "to add to the primitive myth any element which pleases him," the dramatist creates in *Pasiphaé* (1928) a heroine whose action represents a negation of the morality of her time and her people in favor of a strong, individual desire. Dramatic interest results from the crisis she must pass through before she can assert herself.

"Which he desires to commit" is the key phrase in Montherlant's conception. When his heroine announces that she has abandoned herself to the force surging within her and has resolved on acting, she notes, "This day is one which will see me commit an act which I desire to." (112) The emphasis is on individual volition. One of the ways in which Montherlant modernized the myth is by eliminating the divine compulsion and substituting human motives for action. Nowhere does Pasiphaé mention the name of Poseidon or accuse him of being the source of her torments. In making his heroine personally responsible for what befalls her, the contemporary dramatist followed the method so well employed by Racine, particularly in *Phèdre*. However, Montherlant's task was, in one sense at least, much more difficult than that of the French classical dramatist because of the nature of the material available to him. The situation in *Phèdre*, a woman in love with her husband's son, is closer to reality and far less repulsive than that of *Pasiphaé*. What gives the modern drama a universal significance is the fact that Montherlant focuses on the motive rather than the act itself. Like his seventeenth-century predecessor, he does not concern himself solely with brute emotion; the emotion leads towards a clarification of self, a clarification arrived at through suffering.

When Pasiphaé announces her decision to act, she adds, "Today, I put off death." (112) The line is a clue to her deepest convictions and the forces that drive her. Pasiphaé's drama celebrates a rebellion against pressures that threaten her individuality. She reacts against a present reality she finds unbearable. The reality, in her case, is a social one, comprised of restrictions regulating moral conduct, those limitations defined by the author as "the codified opinion of the moment." They result from certain prejudices and customs of the time and place. Pasiphaé's difficulty is that she cannot share such an opinion, for to do so would be to surrender her freedom to the social order. Society, to preserve its unity, demands the likemindedness of its members: The social mind is a synthesis of individual minds. Pasiphaé, however, is conscious of an irreconcilable difference between herself and the social majority, which makes it impossible for her to submit to its views. She protests that her feelings go deeper than do those of most people: "To really love, to really suffer, to really desire — everyone chatters about that as if they knew it all, and the majority hardly suspect what it is all about." (112)

To recognize the difference between one's feelings and those of the majority is one step removed from questioning the source of whatever limitation society imposes to restrict those feelings. Pasiphaé is moved to ask, "Who commanded this restriction? Where is it written? No, no, no restrictions!" (114) What Pasiphaé is questioning, in effect, is social law, that order necessarily limiting the individual's right to pursue his exclusive interest. Some idea of the law that Pasiphaé subscribes to is given to us by Michel Mohrt, who, speaking of Pasiphaé's creator, notes that the morality that Montherlant himself accepted, in essence, was "a personal morality that could be summed up in this sentence: "I have only my idea of self to keep me afloat on the sea of nothingness." [2] The critic adds, "There is only an innate law, written deep within us." In similar language, Pasiphaé justifies her act: "Deep within me I do not believe that what I am about to do is evil." (117) Ultimate reality resides within the individual. He alone, aided by some internal

guide, must regulate his actions. Any attempt by others to
interfere with that activity is an infringement upon his freedom. There is no question of whether the act itself is good or
bad in terms of any absolute concept of morality. What is
important, of course, is that the society that surrounds Pasiphaé
considers it bad.

The only absolute that exists is the individual himself. He
is the locus of worth, dignity, authority, and will. To recognize
him as a law unto himself, however, is to recognize the fact
that there are as many laws as there are individuals. Social
disorder is inevitable. Therefore society must censure the man
who resists relinquishing his freedom in the interests of public
order.

In his brief drama Montherlant made use of the figure of
the Nurse to mirror society's disapproving eye. After Pasiphaé
confides in her and describes the nature of her passion, the
unhappy queen realizes that her Nurse is too social and conventional a being to understand her, and she notices, "It is your
horrified expression, Nurse, and that which all will have, that
creates the evil and makes me guilty, even in my own eyes."
(117) Loyal to her mistress, as such characters are wont to be,
the Nurse nonetheless cannot help expressing her horror, and
as Pasiphaé speaks, she abruptly turns her head. The queen is
finally moved to say, "Since I began speaking with you, you
have not looked at me once." (114)

Society may reject Pasiphaé, but the rejection is mutual.
Montherlant's rebellious heroine says "no" to society by saying
"no" to the reward that awaits those who give up their freedom.
She refutes the ordinary happiness common to blissful lovers
who enjoy the smiles and encouragement of those about them.
She even spurns the peace and contentment of those who are
fortunate enough not to be in love. Comparing her plight to
these lovers and nonlovers alike, she notes, "There is no connection between us. I am not of their kind." (118) That sense
of separation from others that Pasiphaé experiences increases
as the drama proceeds until the queen reaches the point where

she can only repeat, "Here I am alone with my acts. I am so very alone." (119)

It would be an error to regard Pasiphaé as an egoist bent only on satisfying some lust which she insists on rationalizing, objectifying, and glorifying to the exclusion and detriment of all revered rules of human conduct. She is, in fact, quite sensitive to society's condemnation and has made, like Racine's heroine, a valiant effort to struggle against the passion that overwhelms her. Using images that recall the language of the French classical tragedy, Montherlant has the Nurse admit that her mistress no longer welcomes the light of day. Pasiphaé herself compares the fierceness of her struggle to that of a tiny fish who, attempting to swim against a rapid current, finds himself unable to move, held for a moment immobile and powerless by the force of the water until he is finally carried away like a leaf. The drama is an exploration of this moment of immobility during which Pasiphaé is assailed by doubts and torments. Confidence in her decision gives way to hesitation as she recoils at her Nurse's horror. Terribly unhappy because she knows the consequences of her act, she falters at the very last moment. In her final speech she confesses, "Sometimes during moments of weakness, I am seized with the temptation to betray myself into becoming more like the others and sharing a happiness which is not mine. And to defend myself against this temptation, I find only myself, always myself." (122) Despite her momentary weakness, however, Pasiphaé's affirmation that she alone can defend herself against the temptation to share the happiness of others is a declaration of faith in the power of the individual to sustain himself in a menacing world. In her resolution to maintain her convictions, she displays the wisdom of those who know that to betray one's deepest feelings is to live a lifetime of regrets.

Actually, Pasiphaé is not entirely correct when she says that she is alone in her defense. Approval comes from another source — the Chorus. Representing "the intellect which judges," as opposed to a subjective Pasiphaé, the Chorus, instead of discouraging her passion (as one would expect from the voice of the intellect), denounces the queen for considering herself trapped. During one of her moments of irresolution, the unhappy woman speaks of being enclosed in a cage, and the Chorus answers her: "Unhappy, yes unhappy! Not for being encaged, but for believing yourself to be. Unhappy, yes, unhappy, to fly against barriers which do not exist." (115) In a number of instances, the Chorus repeatedly notes that it is not a person's acts that are to be condemned but the person himself if he suffers the judgment of others. Montherlant spends some time discussing the function of the chorus in his Preface to the play. He explains that he approved of the idea of the role being played in evening dress, for such a representation emphasizes the fact that the pronouncements of the Chorus have as much validity today as they had for an audience of thousands of years ago. Moreover, a Chorus in modern dress adds to the impression that what is transpiring on stage is universal enough to occur in our own time.

*Pasiphaé* is a fragmentary drama, originally intended as part of a larger work. Understandably, then, it is short. Much of the work's very sparseness is intentional, however. Action is eliminated in an effort to achieve the static quality of Greek drama. Despite its apparent shortcomings, the work is an interesting one for our study due to Montherlant's depiction of his heroine's struggle. Rebellion is no novelty in the theater. One finds it in all its fierceness in Aeschylus, yet it is a commonplace that the image of Prometheus dominates the modern stage. Why such an image should bear such significance becomes apparent when we scrutinize the makeup of the society our modern plays reflect. The tendency of the individual to become lost in the crowd, a development that appeared so ominous to John Stuart Mill over a century ago, is more pervasive in our technological society of the twentieth century. Today economic influences couple with social factors to render modern man little more than an object in a vast industrialized collective. In many instances, he begins to have a sense of his own meaninglessness within the vastness of a terrifying cosmos the order of which he fails to detect. His sole defense against such dehumanization is to affirm his individual integrity. The heroes and heroines of the works discussed in this chapter are typical of a good many figures in our current plays: they find solace within their own vision of reality from the incongruities of the life which surrounds them. Leading solitary rebellions in the name of individual convictions, they fail noticeably to offer any alternatives to aid in solving the problems that confront them.

The legend of Antigone inspired another dramatist to write a drama of rebellion. In *Antigone* (1942) Jean Anouilh creates a character who shares much with Pasiphaé. Shouting defiance in the face of those forces in life that render insignificant man's sense of his own uniqueness, Antigone echoes Pasiphaé's cries for personal freedom, free of compromise and illumined by the ideal of individual fulfillment. As in Montherlant's drama the force that Anouilh's heroine confronts is explored less for itself than for the occasion it presents for the revelation of self. Cut off from a benevolent deity, isolated by the extremity of her views from her fellow men, and confronted by overwhelming odds, Antigone is sustained by her convictions. Like the unhappy Cretan queen, she displays a firmness that is rare. Anouilh had created the rebel figure in earlier plays, but in the previous works he had concerned himself with the individual's revolt against some particular grievance in his personal situation. With the return to myth, Anouilh began to view the revolt as one possessing universal significance, for now it was directed against the entire human condition. Such a view has dominated his theater ever since. *Antigone* is a powerful work that gains much of its strength from its mythological base. Fundamentally, the ancient story tells of a clash between two human beings, each of whom seeks to affirm the right as he sees it. Anouilh's drama, which is devoid of any intricate plot development, is a depiction of that clash as it occurs. This French drama is structured much like the Sophoclean *Antigone*. Like his Greek counterpart, the modern Créon is a representative of state power over individual necessity. He argues for a life or order; Antigone leads a private rebellion against that order.

Speaking of the rebellion of the Greek Antigone, Albert Camus observes that her rebellion is carried out for the sake of tradition. It occurs to insure her brothers' final resting place, in observance of the rites. In a certain sense her revolt is reactionary.[3] Unlike the classical heroine, Anouilh's Antigone is a rebel against the present, against what Créon has established as the status quo. That reality is so intolerable that she chooses death rather than a life defined according to Créon's edicts.

When Antigone tells Créon, "I am not obliged to do what I do not wish to do,"[4] she is admitting that she has, like Montherlant's heroine a very personal criteria for differentiating right from wrong. Such an attitude has been leading her into difficulties all her life. Ismène tells her, "You are always defying everyone." (155) Ismène would know, for as an older sister she has watched Antigone grow up. Anouilh's treatment of the heroine's passive sister is an interesting example of the way in which the French dramatist worked upon his material. Given some glimpse of the early years of the Theban princess, we discover a classical example of sibling rivalry. Antigone reminds her, "When I was little, I was so mischievous. Do you remember? I used to hurl dirt at you and throw worms down your back." (139) Ismène serves, as she has always done, as a sober contrast to her sister. In addition to her traditional role, she also performs a most important function in drawing Antigone out with regard to those memories she retains of her childhood. When Ismène begs her to try to understand Créon, Antigone retorts:

> Comprendre . . . Vous n'avez que ce mot-là dans la bouche, tous, depuis que je suis toute petite. Il fallait comprendre qu'on ne peut pas toucher à l'eau, à la belle eau fuyante et froide parce que cela mouille les dalles, à la terre parce que cela tache les robes. Il fallait comprendre qu'on ne doit pas manger tout à la fois, donner tout ce qu'on a dans ses poches

au mendiant qu'on rencontre, courir, courir dans le vent jusqu'à
ce qu'on tombe par terre et boire quand on a chaud et se baig-
ner quand il est trop tôt ou trop tard, mais pas juste quand on
en a envie!

Understand! That's the only word I've heard from any of you
ever since I was a child. I had to understand that one must
not play with water — lovely, cold water — because it spills
on the floor. Or with the earth, because it dirties one's clothes.
I had to understand that one must not eat everything at once.
Or give away everything in one's pockets to beggars. Or race
with the wind until you fall to the ground; or drink when you
perspire; or go swimming when it's too soon or too late, just
because you feel like it. (141–2)

Impulsiveness and spontaneity of conduct characterized the
young Antigone. She did what she felt like doing. To the
adults surrounding her she was regarded as a disobedient child,
for she insisted upon following her own rules and disregarding,
like her Greek counterpart, the golden one of adulthood — moderation. The Antigone we meet in the play is essentially the
same being who wanted to eat everything on the dinner table
at once. So she screams at Créon, "I want everything out of
life — right now! And I want it totally! If I can't have it all, I
refuse it. I do not want to be moderate." (180) Her universe,
like that of the child, is bounded by her own desires.

Unlike the child who is ignorant of the world he will one
day grow into, however, Antigone has looked into the hearts
of the adults about her and has reacted against them. She has
reacted against their submissiveness to a life that denies them
their individuality, that levels them to the point where they
become the masses. She knows that in few relationships among
human beings is the individual as important as in the love relationship, yet the kind of love that exalts the beloved above all
others — that even sees uniqueness in an individual's common
name — that creates, in essence, a whole world of one being
seems doomed to failure in this life. Such love is regarded as
romantic and adolescent — something to be tolerated as a phase

one goes through, requiring only the looming oppositions of family, career, or any number of other considerations to kill it. Antigone is repulsed by the thought of lovers who have grown so indifferent to one another that each is no longer so important as to be the center of the other's universe. To advance this favorite theme of the impossibility in life of a surviving love, Anouilh found an ideal springboard in the Antigone-Haemon story with its conclusion in the tragic death of the lovers. The French dramatist develops the love interest to the point where he even describes the engagement of Antigone and the young prince. Scenes are included in which they declare their feelings for one another; details are added that give them a reality much beyond that of lovers in a legend. Further, when Antigone addresses Hémon's father, she confesses that what she admires most about the young man is that he has thus far resisted life's attempts to sully the purity and intensity of their love. If, however, he were to become like the others who say "yes" to life with its compromise happiness, then their love would be destroyed. She tells Créon:

> Si Hémon ne doit plus pâlir quand je pâlis, s'il ne doit plus me croire morte quand je suis en retard de cinq minutes, s'il ne doit plus se sentir seul au monde et me détester quand je ris sans qu'il sache pourquoi, s'il doit devenir près de moi le monsieur Hémon, s'il doit apprendre à dire "oui" lui aussi, alors je n'aime plus Hémon!

> If Haemon were no longer to grow pale when I grow pale; if he were to stop fearing for my life every time I am five minutes late; if he were no longer to feel himself all alone in the world when I laugh and he doesn't know why; if he were to become "Mister" Haemon to me and learn to say "yes" to everything — then I would no longer love him. (187)

The world's indifference and lack of recognition of the purity of love is graphically illustrated in the final tragic moments of the guard scene where Antigone dictates to an insensitive guard a farewell letter intended for Hémon. Led off to her death by Créon's lackeys, she does not even have a chance to utter Hémon's name when the guard asks to whom the letter is to be sent.

The aforementioned scene is significant for its view of ordinary humanity in the person of the guard who jabbers incessantly about such things as his petty material concerns and the rivalry between the Theban army and the palace Guard.[5] Like Pasiphaé during the final moments of her drama, Antigone remarks, "I am all alone." (200) The statement signifies more than a cry of despair at her failure. The modern Antigone, like her Sophoclean counterpart, has sunk to the depths of loneliness, but it is a loneliness to which she has become accustomed. Always conscious of a sense of separation between herself and those she has defied, which is to say the whole world, she recalls Pasiphaé's dreams of another country of extraordinary beings that exists alongside the ordinary world when she tells Créon, "I am far removed from you now, speaking to you of a land which you can no longer enter with your wrinkles, your prudence, your paunch." (187)

Some idea of what this kingdom is like is given to us in the first moments of the drama when Antigone appears, immediately after performing the forbidden ritual. She had gotten up in the early hours of the morning to go out and bury her brother. As she walked towards her destination, she was conscious of the fact that she was the first person out of doors, and she was thrilled and exhilarated. To be the first person out in the morning, to be the first to walk through dewy fields is to have the sensation, for a few brief moments, that one is alone in the world. Nature in all its untouched loveliness existed for her alone at that instant. She tells the nurse, "The garden was still sleeping. I surprised it, Nurse. I came upon it, in all it's beauty, when it was not yet thinking of men." (134)

The kingdom she cherishes is one that is close to the natural world, a pure expanse uninhabited and unsullied by the spoilers, the men with their governments and rules and edicts. It is a world where one can walk through untrampled fields to a desired destination and not meet with any artificial impediments along the way. It is, as Leonard Pronko has pointed out, the world of childhood, a lost paradise of purity.[6] Only when man is a child does he enter such a realm, for only then is he close to nature, a free spirit still unconditioned to the corrupting ways of the society of his elders. The theme is not a particularly original one, having been treated, for example, by myriads of romantic poets. Originality results from the fact that the theme emerges from a mythological situation where previously considerations about nature and society in the context in which Anouilh deals with them remained dormant. Such is the effect of the author's unique presentation of the thoughts that cross Antigone's mind as, making her way towards the carcass of what was once a man, she leaves the city of Thebes behind her.

The order of the state, or the force Antigone rebels against, is more clearly defined than is the order against which Montherlant's heroine rebels, for Anouilh was able to represent it in the towering figure of Créon, his heroine's traditional opponent. In the Greek tragedy the attitude of the successor to the throne of Oedipus is notably different from that of his modern counterpart. It is partially expressed in a number of recurring images drawn from military objects and procedures, as Robert F. Goheen has demonstrated in his excellent *The Imagery of Sophocles' Antigone*. Presented as a military governor, the Sophoclean Créon demands an absolute obedience, which is "characteristic of a military mode of thought when carried beyond its proper provinces."[7] Antigone's rebellion is against an autocratic kind of authority. A modern parallel to the Greek Créon would be the retired army general who attempts to exercise the same control over members of his family or his employees that he exerted over the men who served under him. Anouilh's ruler, however, is not such a figure. A major change in the French drama is the growth in stature of Créon. The modern character resembles the political leader who knows the value of compromise. If he occasionally resorts to "arm-twisting" methods, it is less because he seeks absolute control and more because he seeks his goal, a peaceful and tranquil society, and he makes noteworthy efforts to avoid the tragedy. In rebelling against such a figure, the modern Antigone revolts against the entire political-social structure.

Créon considers life worthwhile if he can work successfully at what he considers to be his trade, that of ruling the citizens of his state. Saying "yes" to life means rolling up one's sleeves and doing whatever unpleasant tasks life places before one. As king of Thebes, Créon's task is to introduce order into a kingdom made chaotic by the deeds of Oedipus and his revolutionary sons. In the interests of that order individual volition must be subordinated to the larger good. Créon's description of how a leader creates domestic tranquility betrays his distrust of the individual:

> On prend le bout de bois, on redresse devant la montagne d'eau, on gueule un ordre et on tire dans le tas, sur le premier qui s'avance. Dans le tas! Cela n'a pas de nom. C'est comme la vague qui vient de s'abattre sur le pont devant nous; le vent qui vous gifle, et la chose qui tombe dans le groupe n'a pas de nom. C'était peut-être celui qui t'avait donné du feu en souriant la veille. Il n'a plus de nom. Et toi non plus, tu n'as plus de nom, cramponné à la barre. Il n'y a plus que le bateau qui ait un nom et la tempête.

> One grabs the wheel, rights the ship in the path of a mountain of water, shouts an order, and, when the first man disobeys, fires into the pack. Into the pack! The thing which drops in the midst of the crowd has no name. He is like the sea that floods the deck on which you stand; the wind that smacks against your face. He could be the man with whom you talked and laughed the night before. He no longer has a name. And you, grasping the helm, you no longer have a name. Only the ship and the storm have a name. (180)

In denying a man his name, Créon is denying that which sets him apart from other men. Antigone tells him that he would make a good king, if only men were animals. However Créon feels justified because the end he seeks results from his tactics. Happiness is achieved by compromising one's personal desires to the demands of life. This is exactly what Créon has done himself. The Chorus reveals the following:

Avant, du tempe d'Oedipe, quand il n'était que le premier personnage de la cour, il aimait la musique, les belles reliures, les longues flâneries chez les petits antiquaires de Thèbes. Mais Oedipe et ses fils sont morts. Il a laissé ses livres, ses objets, il a retroussé ses manches et il a pris leur place.

Years ago, in the days of Oedipus, when he was only the king's relative, he loved music and rare books. He liked to spend hours browsing in the antique shops of Thebes. But Oedipus and his sons died. And he left his books and his objects of art, rolled up his sleeves, and went to work in their place. (132)

Créon himself tells Antigone, "Kings have other things to do than to surrender to private sentiments, my dear girl." (171)

When Antigone defies Créon's edict, she is acting on behalf of the individual and his right to fulfill himself. No doubt were she to formulate her thoughts within the framework of a political philosophy, she would find herself agreeing with John Stuart Mill that the state that dwarfs its men so that they may become docile instruments in its hands, even for beneficial purposes, soon finds that with small men, no great things can ever be accomplished. Nevertheless, Créon knows that if each person were to pursue his individual needs, chaos would result. Society is sustained by order, and to believe that the order could be disrupted to indulge the wishes of one person without interfering with the pursuits of others is to believe in a utopian fantasy.

What is clear is that both Créon and Antigone are pursuing the same evasive goal that all men seek, happiness. The difficulty is that they have opposing views on how it can be obtained. Créon speaks for compromise and Antigone for purity. In order to emphasize the similarity between the two and the fact that they are both doomed to be frustrated in their wishes, Anouilh includes repeated references to the tragic history of the family to which they both belong. Créon may berate Antigone with the words, "Keep it up! Keep it up! Like your father." (188) but one is also reminded that Créon was the former king's brother-in-law. Also, another method used by the dramatist to heighten the similarity between the two is the characterization of Créon. Anouilh's figure may be more humane and clearsighted than his Greek counterpart, as Leonard Pronko points out,[8] but he is also a good deal more stubborn than the character who is finally persuaded by the prophecy of Teiresias to alter his edict, hard though it may be, and give Polynices burial and Antigone freedom. Anouilh's character demonstrates no such change of heart. True, there is no Teiresias, with his divine contacts, in the modern drama; but the urgings of Hémon and the Chorus would persuade a less obstinate man. In his persisting stubbornness he most resembles Antigone.

Try as he will, what Créon cannot understand about Antigone is what her rebellion signifies. He is familiar enough with rebellion, but the only rebel he has encountered thus far has been the political rebel. Thus when he first hears from the frightened guard that the corpse has been buried, his first reaction is to believe that friends of Polynices have accomplished the deed, and he mutters to himself, "A crushed rebellion which is already gathering new strength." (159) Even when he finally confronts Antigone — and he admits that he has imagined that the person confronting him in such a situation would be a pale young assassin — he cannot comprehend her motive. If any facial expression characterizes Créon during the great debate scene, it is surely that of open-mouthed disbelief, with occasional lapses into confidence — the lapses becoming more infrequent as the drama progresses. During one such moment of confidence, the king betrays his total incapacity to understand his niece when he tells her,

> Je ne veux pas te laisser mourir dans une histoire de politique. Tu vaux mieux que cela. Parce que ton Polynice, cette ombre éplorée et ce corps qui se décompose entre ses gardes et tout ce pathétique qui t'enflamme, ce n'est qu'une histoire de politique.

> I won't have you fall victim to a political affair. You are worth more than that. For this whole matter of Polynices: this mournful specter, this guarded, decomposing body, and all

these sentiments which stir you — is nothing more than politics. (176)

Créon believes that the whole business is simply a matter of politics. And he is worried about his career.

Créon is a realist and he leaves out no details in his characterization of the sons of Oedipus. The description of the boys is a further instance of the way in which Anouilh modernized the myth for his own purposes. To begin with, the reference to Eteocles and Polynices frequenting night clubs is one of a number of anachronistic details that Anouilh introduced into the drama. Such additions serve to bring the myth close to everyday reality. In addition, Créon's informative remarks introduce certain innovations in regard to the characterization of the mythological figures. The young princes, as the French dramatist presents them, were prodigals, each intent on his own gains and totally unworthy of any tears. There is a suggestion that Antigone admired the independent airs of her big brothers, who were often unruly and drunk. Créon reminds her that she looked up to her brothers admiringly when a youngster, but what she truly admired was a gesture. After returning from one of his evenings out, Polynices gave her a big paper flower he had brought home for her, and Antigone preserved that flower. The action is a clue to her idealism, to the fact that she could preserve her faith in the face of great opposition. Créon is able to shake that idealism only once: when he reveals that both brothers were scoundrels and that he is not sure which corpse was given a state funeral and which was left unburied.

Thoroughly disarmed by such revelations, Antigone recants. She yields to the temptation that Pasiphaé felt to give up her cause. What recalls her to her purpose is Créon's confession that he too was once an idealist. Faced with the spectacle of an idealist turned "cook," as she prefers to call the king, Anouilh's heroine suddenly has a glimpse of what her life will be if she follows the "cook's" advice. She will turn into a duplicate of Créon, betraying her innermost convictions and subscribing to a life of practical realities. She knows finally what she has suspected throughout her debate with her uncle, that he is guilty of self-deception.

Créon's technique throughout the scene with Antigone is to challenge all her beliefs until he can bring her to the point where she will recant, and he is successful, though only for the brief moment referred to above. Earlier he had succeeded in obtaining the admission that her motive in performing the sacred rite had not been a religious one. In considering the extent to which Anouilh transformed his material, the question of Antigone's motive is one of the first to arise. A popular view has it that the modern Antigone differs from her Greek (which, in this case, is to say her Sophoclean) counterpart in that the classical Antigone acts in obeisance to a religious law whereas Anouilh's heroine acts out of personal motives. However, a close examination of the play reveals, as it did to H. D. F. Kitto, that Sophocles himself altered the religious motive. Kitto argues that Antigone's real thought comes out in phrases such as "He has no right to touch what is *mine!*" Gradually, he notes, her defenses fail one by one until she is left with the fact that she did it and she had to do it. The tone is personal.[9] Thus when Anouilh's heroine tells Créon that she acted "for no one. For myself," she is giving evidence of the fact that the French dramatist developed an idea already present in the Sophoclean drama. Where his version of the tale differs from that of Sophocles is not so much the fact that his heroine rejects a religious motive but that she rejects religion altogether. When Créon ridicules the ministrations of the priests and debunks the belief concerning the necessity of burial, he uses one word to summarize the entire religious mechanism — and it is the word that Antigone repeats — "absurd." The modern Antigone no longer believes, as her Greek counterpart did, that there is a divine order with which she can become reconciled, even at the expense of tragic suffering. The Sophoclean heroine may or may not have a religious motive, but she does not consider herself cut off from the cosmic order. Even if she can be detected questioning that order when in the depths of despair, such doubt is indicative of little more than a temporary lapse of faith, something that is experienced regularly by the most religious of people.

Regardless of motive, however, one must agree that the importance of the act itself remains. To consider the act merely a pretext for wilful action, as Créon does, is to accuse Antigone of that deception that usually accompanies the use of pretexts. For a purist like Antigone, such deception is distasteful. Rather, it may be more accurate to speak of the burial of Polynices as the occasion for the self-asserting action; that is not to say that another occasion would not do as well, but that the myth provided the artist with the one he made use of, just as Montherlant used Pasiphaé's sudden seizure of passion for a bull as the occasion for his heroine's overt defiance of the society against which she rebels.

The king's first error is to disregard human feelings. His second is to believe that he can reconstruct Fate. He has his own plans for Antigone; possessing a good deal of farsightedness, he sees himself as head of a dynasty that his niece will help propagate. Fate, however, has ordained that Antigone will die. Actually, the question of the extent to which Anouilh wished to portray Antigone's life as fated is somewhat confused. Leonard Pronko notes that in assigning man a role to play, the author introduces the deterministic note; but in placing his character before a choice, and giving him leeway to act upon that choice, Anouilh seems to suggest that man is free.[10] The whole question of Fate is very much present in the myth, of course. Perhaps one may resolve the confusion by noting that given Antigone's personality structure, some clash of the nature dramatized is inevitable — whether that clash occur with Créon or with someone else like him. Once she meets her adversary, Anouilh's heroine — if she is to be true to herself — will demonstrate predictable behavior.

At any rate, the Chorus, played by a single actor, does do some predicting. Speaking for Anouilh, he introduces and later interrupts the action to tell the tale in advance. His matter of fact, almost nonchalant, style in relating the very tragic events of the play emphasizes what he is trying to convey to the audience: that tragedy is inevitable, restful. By making himself a part of the mythological tale, at least in this respect, Anouilh follows the practice of Montherlant, who also used the device of the Chorus as a means of expressing personal views. Where Montherlant's Chorus is quite verbal in his support of the heroine, though, Anouilh's Chorus seems indifferent to what befalls any of the characters. Only towards the end of the play does he step in and urge Créon to relent and save his niece. For the most part he confines his comments to reflections on the nature of tragedy. One such comment informs us that tragedy is like some infernal machine in perfect order: "The spring is coiled. It will simply unwind itself." (160) Because tragedy is inevitable, hope has no part in it.

Hope has no part in this particular tragedy for a specific reason. Hope is rejected by the heroine. Speaking of her father as well as of herself, Antigone tells Créon, "We are among those who can live without hope, your beloved, filthy hope!" (188) Hope is filthy because it is deceitful; because it leads you to believe that things will turn out well for you when logic tells you they will not; because, finally, it suspends you midway between joy and despair, allowing you (at the very most) a false happiness — a happiness remembered in bitterness when you finally realize that you are defeated. Antigone becomes like Camus' man of the Absurd; she forsakes hope, for she has no belief in an ultimate justice within this world. She knows what the Chorus predicts — that her death is inevitable. Hope is reserved for those like T. S. Eliot's hero, Harry, who can look to the future confident that, whatever trials they must endure, there is an order to which man can find a place, an order that will grant him everlasting freedom and life.

Antigone differs from those who have no faith in eternity in one respect; she does not fear physical death. She scorns all opportunities Créon offers her to save herself. When she confesses, finally, that it is terrible to die and she is frightened, such admissions cannot be taken seriously as an indication that she has changed her basic attitude. Rather, they are evidence of the fact that despite her rigid stand she is, after all, quite human. If she does concede anything to Créon, she offsets that concession by hanging herself. It is undeniable that her attitude is nihilistic, but she exhibits a nihilism characteristic of a certain type of rebel, a type which Albert Camus understood. He explains:

> On peut être nihiliste de deux façons, et chaque fois par une intempérance d'absolu. Il y a apparemment les révoltés qui veulent mourir et ceux qui veulent faire mourir. Mais ce sont les memes, brûlés du desir de la vraie vie, frustrés de l'être et préférant alors l'injustice généralisée à une justice mutilée.

> One can be a nihilist in two ways, both ways involving an intemperate embracing of absolutes. There are, apparently, rebels who wish to die and those who wish to cause death. But they are the same: consumed with the desire for the true life, frustrated in achieving it, and preferring, as a result, a generalized injustice to a mutilated justice.[11]

Camus, of course, disapproved of this type of revolt. He felt that the nihilistic rebel offers no solution for the ills from which he suffers.

The true life for Antigone is the life of the spirit; the only death she fears is the death of her freedom, of her right to be true to herself. Her physical death is merely the means by which she preserves her ideals. She is frustrated, of course, because she does want to live, yet she cannot make the necessary compromise which will assure her a few years longer on earth. She brings destruction to others; the Chorus notes, "If not for Antigone, it is true, they would all have been left at peace." (206) Nevertheless, her resolution in the face of great opposition is a manifestation of her great courage. Her heroism is that of the individual who can tear himself away from a status quo existence that is much more comfortable and cheaper, in many respects, than a life of commitment to one's true beliefs. If it is her tragedy to die, the tragedy is surely that of the world that permits its idealists, its visionaries, to despair. Antigone's vision may lack moderation, but what is admirable is the totality with which she applies herself to its cause. There are very few Antigones in our society. Most people lack the honesty and the capacity to disrupt their comfortable, ordered existences when they discover that their true feelings conflict with the lives they are leading. Rather, they go on with their day-to-day routine, interrupted only by an occasional memory or a deep sigh for what might have been. Having missed the great challenges and adventures in living, they remain like Anouilh's guards: "They continue to play cards."

For Jean Giraudoux the image of the rebel was distinguishable among Agamemnon's unhappy brood. In the violent opposition of the daughter of the Greek king to the enemies of her father, Giraudoux found an opportunity to record the protest of a girl who, like the figures previously discussed in this chapter, strikes out in the name of individual integrity. The target of the heroine of *Electre* (1937), though dramatized in the shape of the usurper of Agamemnon's throne, would be recognizable to Pasiphaé and to Antigone. It resolves itself into that view of reality which accepts a compromise happiness, subordinating private interests to some larger structure and rendering idealism a type of fanaticism. To capitulate to that view is to lose sight of a self-image that would enable one to define himself within the chaos of existence.

Electra's rebelliousness issues from a sense of disquiet concerning her father's death and disdain for his successor. Continually she expresses her rejection of the rulers of Argos by going every night to pay homage at the tomb of the dead king. No edicts exist to restrict such activity, but Electra's behavior disturbs Egisthe. She is, he believes, a threat to the security of the city by her indulgence in a practice which Egisthe defines as "signaling to the gods." In response to a request for an explanation of the term, Egisthe volunteers the following:

C'est se séparer de la troupe, monter sur une éminence, et agiter sa lanterne ou son drapeau. On trahit la terre comme

on trahit une place assiégée, par des signaux. Le philosophe
les fait, de sa terrasse, le poète ou le désespéré les fait, de son
balcon ou de son plongeoir. Si les dieux depuis dix ans, n'ar-
rivent point à se mêler de notre vie, c'est que j'ai veillé, à ce
que les promontoires soient vides et les champs de foire
combles, c'est que j'ai ordonné le mariage des rêveurs, des
peintres et des chimistes; c'est que, pour éviter de créer entre
nos citoyens ces différences de race morale qui ne peuvent
manquer de colorer différemment les hommes aux yeux des
dieux, j'ai toujours feint d'attribuer une importance énorme aux
délits et dérisoire aux crimes. Rien n'entretient mieux la fixité
divine que la même atmosphère égale autour des assassinats et
des vols da pain. Je dois reconnaître que sur ce point la justice
des tribunaux m'a abondamment secondé. Et toutes les fois
où j'ai été obligé de sevir, de là-haut on ne l'a point vu. Aucune
de mes sanctions n'a été assez voyante pour permettre aux
dieux l'ajustement de leur vengeance.

It is to separate oneself from the crowd, climb up to some high
ground, and wave a lantern or a flag. One betrays the earth
in the same way as one betrays a besieged fortification, by
signals. The philosopher signals from his terrace, the poet or
the hopeless man from his balcony or his diving-board. If the
gods have failed, for the past ten years, to interfere with our
lives, it is because I have made sure that the promontories are
empty and the fair-grounds crowded; I have ordered all the
dreamers, the artists, and the chemists to marry; and, to avoid
encouraging among our people distinctive moral strains which
render men different in the eyes of the gods, I have always pre-
tended to allot great importance to misdemeanors and absurdly
little to crimes. Nothing is as effective for keeping the gods
impassive as equal punishment for those who murder and for
those who steal a loaf of bread. I must admit that on this
point the courts have strongly supported me. And each time
that I have been obliged to be severe, no one up there noticed
it. None of my sanctions has been so conspicuous that the
gods have had to alter their vengeance.[12]

The courts have supported Egisthe in his determination to
reduce all crimes to the level of misdemeanors, and the citizens
have supported his orders requiring all the visionaries among

them (chemists included) to marry. Marriage is Egisthe's solution to the problem of restless idealism among his subjects.
Having successfully avoided that institution himself, he now
plans to marry off the restless Electre to the palace gardener.

Giraudoux has made use of the Euripidean version of the
myth, that which recounts the marriage of Electra to a humble
gardener, in order to demonstrate the kind of tyranny the
usurper-king exercises over Agamemnon's daughter. What interests the French author is not so much the fact that the
marriage is a forced one, but Egisthe's reason for desiring the
match. Electre alone among the people of Argos perpetuates
the memory of Agamemnon. She has separated herself from
the crowd by her refusal to follow the general tendency to
forget the past. Egisthe explains what he hopes to accomplish
by the marriage:

> Je ne dissimule point qu'Electre m'inquiète. Je sens que les
> ennuis et les malheurs abonderont du jour où elle se déclarera,
> comme tu dis, dans la famille des Atrides. Et pour tous, car
> tout citoyen est atteint de ce qui frappe la famille royale. C'est
> pour cela que je la passe à une famille invisible des dieux,
> amorphe, et dans laquelle ni ses yeux ni ses gestes n'auront
> plus de phosphore, où le ravage restera local et bourgeois, à la
> famille des Théocathoclès.

> I am not concealing the fact that Electra makes me uneasy. I
> believe that problems and misfortunes will vex the Atreidae
> family from the day she reveals herself, as you put it. And
> everyone will be affected, since everyone is influencd by what
> happens to the royal family. For this reason I am placing her
> in a family which is formless, invisible to the gods, one in which
> her eyes and her gestures will lose their phosphorescence, and
> the devastation will be local and bourgeois — contained in the
> Théocathoclès family. (30)

By reducing Agamemnon's daughter to the status of a married
member of the middle class, he hopes to snuff out her individuality. He seeks to do what Créon failed to do to Antigone and
what society could not accomplish with Pasiphaé. The same

attempt at leveling, or causing the subject to become apathetic and "average" is in evidence.

Electre will continue to stir up trouble, however, because she is opposed to forgetfulness and compromise. She is implacable. Rejecting, like Anouilh's heroine, what she considers to be a sham happiness — since it is founded on the principle of compromise — she plays out the role that the myth has always assigned to her — that of the woman who waits for the moment when she will realize her dream of vengeance. She tells Clytemnestre, "The only happiness I have known in this world is waiting." (77) Aware of the fact that her beliefs differ radically from those about her, she is, like the modern Antigone, content only when taking solitary morning walks. She confesses that what she has been doing during these walks is waiting for the spirit of her father to rise, as in the legend the spirit of the dead Agamemnon rose in response to the prayers of his children for revenge. Speaking in Giraudoux's beautiful prose, she tells Clytemnestre:

> A part toi, à part les hommes, il n'était rien dans le palais qui n'attendît mon père avec moi, qui ne fût complice ou partie dans mon attente. Cela commençait le matin, mère, à ma première promenade sous ces tilleuls qui te haïssent, qui attendaient mon père d'une attente qu'ils essayaient vainement de comprimer en eux, vexés de vivre par années et non comme il l'aurait fallu, par décades, hontaux de l'avoir trahi à chaque printemps quand ils ne pouvaient plus, contenir leurs fleurs et leurs parfums, et qu'ils défaillaient avec moi sur son absence. . . . où j'attends encore, où j'attends la passé, où je l'attends encore!

> Aside from you and the others, everything in this palace was my accomplice in waiting for my father. It began in the morning, Mother, during my early walk beneath the linden trees that detest you. They were waiting for my father with an expectation which they tried in vain to suppress, being vexed at having to live by the years rather than by the decades, as they should. They were ashamed at having to betray him each spring when they could no longer withold their blossoms

and their fragrance from the world — heartsick, like me, at his absence.

. . . when I still wait, when I wait for the past, when I still wait! (78)

A rebel against the present, Electre's protest occurs in the name of the past, which remains alive in her. By refusing to forget, it is she who keeps the sins of the past alive. The princess's entire world, moreover, is comprised only of that which accommodates her most fervid wish. Separated from the world of men, it is only with the world of nature and inanimate objects that she detects a kinship. Although unaware, at first, of the fact that her father was murdered, she nonetheless waits in expectation for some revelation. Her talent for waiting serves her well. The spirit of Agamemnon finally appears to her in a dream and reveals the sordid tale. The effect of such an innovation is to create a feeling that some Fate is at work to carry the story through to its predictable end — for despite the many original touches that abound in this play, it ends with Oreste's murder of Clytemnestre and Egisthe and his flight from the pursuing Furies. The nature of that Fate is not defined, but it is represented in the figures of the little Eumenides, who also take on the form of the three Fates. Giraudoux postponed the disclosures of the facts of Agamemnon's death until the second half of the play, but in the first act he makes many veiled references to what is to come. One such instance occurs when the three little Fates play at being Oreste and Clytemnestre. The girl playing the role of the queen asks of her player-son, "Have you come to kill me, to kill Aegisthus?" (53)

The first act reveals, moreover, that although Electre has no specific cause for hating Egisthe, she seems to intuit his guilt, as she does that of Clytemnestre. She is unable to accept the present situation, the fact that her father is dead and Egisthe has taken his place, both politically and domestically. Electre is dissatisfied with the *status quo* in her city. The first clash between Egisthe and Electre is one based on a difference in principles. We are told that her ally is "total justice."

As we have seen, Egisthe's philosophy demands of all citizens a subordination of their private interests and dreams to the wishes of the state and an unquestioning acceptance of his view of justice, which is respected by the Argive courts. Electre looks elsewhere for justice; she calls upon the sleeping gods to shake off their torpor and participate in the affairs of men. Such behavior is seditious. Egisthe fears for the future. He fears that the princess will "reveal" herself.[13] Electre's early desire for justice overwhelms her when she discovers the extent of the injustice done to Agamemnon. One of the reasons why the modern heroine expresses her revolt in the form of a protest for absolute justice is that the entire question of justice forms a crucial aspect of the myth. Whereas the opposition in the Greek tale is between old and new conceptions of divine justice, here it is between Egisthe's view and that of Electre. Each character rejects both the other's view and any faith in divine intervention. Electre may signal to the gods, and Egisthe may fear such defiance of his authority, but both know that the influence of divine powers in regard to man's daily affairs is negligible. Egisthe concedes that he has had doubts concerning his belief in the gods and that he has finally come to believe in them not as guardians concerned with their charge, humanity, but as great abstractions forever oscillating between space and time, indifferent to the point that they have reached a state of serenity where their only activity is that of a multifaceted diamond — the silent reflection of light.

There is one representative from Olympus in Argos, the Beggar-God, a pure fabrication of the French dramatist's. Mumbling weighty parables and prophecies, he injects a note of impending gloom, but there is no indication that he drives the characters to action. Electre knows that the gods will not respond when she challenges divine justice to appear before her and absolve Egisthe. Speaking of the tyrant's desire to reform and his new claim to the city as a gift of the heavens, Electre admits, in effect, that she has her own views of the matter: "A splendid repentance for a crime is the verdict which the gods have rendered in your case. I do not accept it." (99) Electre accepts only her own conceptions of justice. Like

Pasiphaé and Antigone, she looks within herself for standards of conduct and values. She advises Egisthe to do likewise: "Just listen to the voice deep within you." (95) Listening to the voice within her own soul and prodding Oreste to action to accomplish her view of justice is Electre's way of realizing what she must do and asserting herself.

While Electra is revealing herself, Egisthe is doing much the same thing. The power of Giraudoux's drama, like Anouilh's work, lies in the fact that the forces that oppose each other are equal in strength and appeal. Remembering, perhaps, that the legendary Aegisthus was not a complete blackguard (for his motive in killing Agamemnon was to avenge the king's murder of his father, Thyestes), the French dramatist makes of Agamemnon's successor a sympathetic character. Further, the presentation of Aegisthus as a political figure of some weight is a development of a latent theme in Sophocles' *Electra*. In the Greek drama the significance of Aegisthus as ruler is made apparent by the fact that his death occurs after that of Clytemnestra, rather than the reverse, which is the case of the Aeschylean and Euripidean versions. Because the most important figure is the last one killed, the implication of the action in Sophocles' play (a surprised Aegisthus being presented with the corpse of Clytemnestra and then being taken inside the palace by Orestes to be slain on the very spot where he slew Agamemnon) is that Aegisthus wields substantial political power.

In the hands of the French dramatist, Aegisthus becomes a dedicated statesman willing to make even the supreme sacrifice — marriage to Clytemnestra — to assure the welfare of his people. Interestingly enough, the stimulant for such a change is rebellion, but it is not Electre's variety of revolt that results in his new outlook. The only rebellion he understands is that which is based on political discontent. Rebels within the city, signaling to the attacking Corinthians outside, present the only threat with which Egisthe is capable of dealing. He is very much like the modern Créon in this regard. Confident that he can restore order, he reveals that he has had a vision of an

Argos rebuilt through his efforts, an alabaster city gleaming in the light of a new dawn. He has become an idealist, and he recognizes the idealism in Electre and begs her for support. Egisthe also seeks truth and abhors his past lies. Tragedy results from the fact that although Electre wishes for the same new dawn she advocates a violent method, a method opposed to that of Egisthe's, for attaining it. Aware of a threat to her city, she tells Egisthe, "We disagree on the nature of the danger." (97) In witholding her support, she renders Egisthe powerless.

The rebellion theme exists alongside the traditional theme of vengeance. Critic Donald Inskip has identified the first theme as "that of the *raison d'état* as opposed to single-minded purity of intention." [14] Failing to note the fact that Electre's refusal to accept Egisthe's rule is a revolt against his view of justice, Inskip goes on to criticize Giraudoux's craftsmanship on the grounds that the simultaneous unfolding of both themes destroys the play's unity, for the effort to link them was beyond the dramatist's power.[15] The development of the rebellion theme is, of course, the new element Giraudoux added to his treatment of the tale. Furthermore because it does indeed take up the question of justice, it is impossible to treat without considering the crime that has created the injustice (and which has resulted in Egisthe's rule). Once he considers the crime, the author is bound, because of the order of the myth, to take up the question of vengeance. It seems to me that the link between the two themes in Giraudoux's play is that Electre's quest for vengeance is one and the same with her quest for absolute justice (and its corollary, absolute truth). The uncovering of the infamous past uncovers the canker that is infecting the Argive society. When Electre comes to know the truth of her father's death, she also comes to realize that Egisthe is sincere in his desire for atonement, but she refuses to forgive him for murdering Agamemnon. The reason for her implacability has to do with her view of the crime, which she considers an infection that has corrupted the nation. In reply to Egisthe's "Does Electra's justice consist of re-sifting every fault, of making every deed irreparable?" she defines the crime: "In some years frost is justice for the trees; in others it is injustice. There are convicts one loves, assassins one embraces. But when a crime injures human dignity, infects a whole people, corrupts their loyalty, it cannot be forgiven." (99)

The contented faces of the Argive citizens Electre sees about her reflect, she believes, a happiness founded on Egisthe's principles:

> Mais, depuis la mort de mon père, depuis que la bonheur de notre ville est fondé sur l'injustice et le forfait, depuis que chacun, par lâcheté, s'y est fait le complice du meurtre et du mensonge, elle peut être prospère, elle peut chanter, danser et vaincre, le ciel peut éclater sur elle, c'est une cave où les yeux sont inutiles.

> Since the moment of my father's death, when the happiness of our city became dependent on injustice and crime, and each person, out of cowardice, became an accomplice to murder and deception — though we prosper, sing, and dance — we have been inhabiting a land of darkness where eyes are useless. (99–100)

Electre's suggestion that all the Argives bear the guilt of Agamemnon's murder, for as supporters of Egisthe they are his accomplices, introduces an idea that Jean-Paul Sartre made use of some six years later in *Les Mouches*. In that play the crime of Egisthe, the unjust ruler, is shared by the people who, possessing the opportunity to save Agamemnon on that fateful day, maintained silence and saw him murdered. The Argives of *Les Mouches*, too, are accomplices who soon see their society made sick by the effect of the crime. (Also, Jupiter's distinction between crimes that pay and those that do not recalls Electre's division of crimes into different categories.) Sartre, too, had to deal with the vengeance theme. In his case, however, he was able to dismiss it quickly enough for his Oreste rejects vengeance as a possible mode of action. The difficulty in Giraudoux's play is that the delayed revelation of the facts of Agamemnon's murder gives rise to a certain amount of ambiguity, for the first half of the drama contains merely hints and guesses about the action to follow. In this respect, interestingly enough, Giraudoux is introducing a method T. S. Eliot was to use two years later when, for different reasons, his Orestes remains ignorant of the facts concerning his father until we are well into Part II of *The Family Reunion*.[16]

Giraudoux's heroine has made the observation that all Argives are accomplices in order to emphasize the fact that she considers herself a guiltless being and an alien in Egisthe's city. Like the heroines of Montherlant and Anouilh, she dreams of a country of her own, apart from the society in which she lives. The vision that Electre has had is of a land where contentment results from the rarefied atmosphere of her own idealistic conceptions. Knowing that her attitude will cause the annihilation of her city and the destruction of Egisthe's plans for reconstruction, she resembles the nihilistic rebel of Camus' definition in her preference for a dead Argos rather than one in which she must make compromises. Thus she tells the pleading Egisthe, "Sometimes the spirit of a dead nation lives forever. Would that such could be the fate of Argos!" (99)

Another innovation of Giraudoux's that appears to disrupt the play's unity because it introduces extraneous material is the inclusion of what may be loosely considered a subplot, the Agathe-Président situation. These characters introduce a note of farce into the tragedy, which appears to disrupt the play's somber tone and introduce an element that seems generally out of place in Electre's story. To exclude such material, though, is to eliminate much of the wit and charm that characterize the author's style. In addition, and more important, the farcical overtones mask a more serious purpose. The story of the flighty Agathe and her husband is linked to the two weighty themes of the work and used by the dramatist to good advantage. In addition to the superficial link of the Théocathoclès family with Electre, by means of the Gardener, Agathe and her deceived husband are the means whereby Electre is aided in her search for the truth about Clytemnestre. The queen's betrayal of jealousy at Agathe's boast that Egisthe is her lover makes a good deal clear to Electre. Further, Agathe and the Président are linked to the rebellion theme because they provide an insight into what it is that Electre revolts against. The Président, who is the first to characterize Electre as implacable while defining her idealism, speaks for the order Egisthe represents. He is the first to speak for forgiveness and compromise. What is significant is that this person who is Egisthe's Chief Justice turns out to be a man who is easily fooled by the transparent actions of his wife. Because of the Président's inability to keep adequate order within his own household, Electre may have every reason to believe that Argive justice is inadequate.

In regard to Clytemnestre, Giraudoux has made of her a shallow woman whose vanity leads her to object to Electre's marriage to the Gardener on the grounds that this worthy man is not her social equal. Incapable of love, the queen shares with Egisthe a relationship that is fast beginning to duplicate that which she experienced with Agamemnon: she and her lover have reached the point where they merely tolerate one another. Despite an occasional clash with Electre, she is hardly a worthy opponent to her daughter. She senses the princess's thoughts — as she demonstrates when she advises her daughter: "Stop acting like a judge, Electre." (75) — but she is incapable of understanding the debate between Egisthe and Electra over large issues. At best she can muster only an irrelevant observation on justice, or the lack of it. Speaking of the days of her trouble-free youth when her innocent pursuits included picking flowers, playing with her dog, and singing gaily, she compares those moments to her present unhappy lot and riles, "What injustice!" (102)

Giraudoux's description of Clytemnestre's relationship with Electre as a child is interesting in that it throws some light on her daughter's personality. The young princess exhibited, like Anouilh's heroine, moments of mischief. What she was like may be surmised from the behavior of the Eumenides who share identities with her. When we first see them they are naughty little girls; apparently, the princess's behavior was similar. In the absence of a besieged older sister, Clytemnestre is present to give evidence of Electre's childhood behavior. Whether or not one believes the queen's story that her daughter pushed the baby Oreste out of his mother's arms, it is true that Electre opposed her from the moment she was born. Clytemnestre relates:

> Nous avons été des indifférentes dès ta première minute. Tu ne m'as même pas fait souffrir à ta naissance. Tu étais menue, réticente. Tu serrais les lèvres. Si un an tu as serré obstiné-ment les lèvres, c'est de peur que ton premier mot ne soit le nom de ta mère. Ni toi ni moi n'avons pleuré ce jour-là. Ni toi ni moi n'avons jamais pleuré ensemble.

> We were indifferent to one another from the moment you were born. You did not even cause me pain at your birth. You were slight, reticent. You kept your lips pressed together. You kept them obstinately shut for an entire year for fear that your first word would be your mother's name. Neither you nor I cried that day. We have never cried together. (76–7)

Without developing any psychological motives for action, Giraudoux suggests that there is something within Electre's personality that creates the attitude of revolt we have examined. Some six years earlier, Eugene O'Neill made use of a similar innovation in *Mourning Becomes Electra*. In the case of O'Neill's play, however, the antagonism between Christine and Lavinia which is developed at the time of the daughter's birth is due to Christine's hatred of her husband. A possible explanation for the early conflict between Giraudoux's characters is that Electre's hatred of her mother and her expressed wish that she could have been born somehow without a natural mother is evidence of the revolt of one generation against the other.[17] Electre's desire to be an orphan appears, in fact, related to that fantasy, common to adolescents who conflict with their parents, that one could not possibly be the natural child of such people and, therefore, one must have been adopted.

Clytemnestre's influence is confined to Oreste. The young prince differs from the legendary hero in that he has no desire for revenge. In making Electre the more aggressive of the two

children of Agamemnon, Giraudoux left to Oreste a more passive role. Ignorant of his father's murder and his mother's deception until enlightened by Electre, he does not return in
search of vengeance. Seeking a life he feels deprived of, he
does not wish to hear of his sister's hatred and sorrow. He
stops Electre with the words, "Let us save our hatred for to-
morrow. This evening let me enjoy, if only for one hour, the
sweetness of this life which I never knew and which now I
regain." (48) He is, like Sartre's hero, nostalgic for a life he
never knew. Where Electre is gloomy, Oreste is gay; he likes
to dress well and laugh a good deal. Such is the way he would
like to remain in Argos. Eager to believe only good things of
his mother, he is easily swayed by her protests of innocence
and even begs the queen, at one point, to convince him that
Electre lies. He falls into an untroubled harmony with his
surroundings and would accept a compromise happiness.
Oreste wishes to take his unhappy sister away from Argos. He
wishes to show her his rose and jasmin covered house in Thessaly. The princess can only ridicule him. A witness to Clytemnestre's greeting of the young man as "My Son . . . Handsome. Regal." (51) Electre mocks his reluctance to act: "You
are like all other men, Oreste! They give way to the least
flattery; they are won over by the least attention." (70) Eventually, Electre has her way and Oreste goes off to stab his
mother and Egisthe. Even then, however, his reluctance is
apparent in the fact that he strikes blindly, his eyes closed.

The Eumenides who try to dissuade Oreste are an example
of Giraudoux's highly original treatment. They change as the
drama progresses. But they do not change from dread pur-
suers to kindly spirits as in the legend, for there is no reconciliation with a benign order at the end of this drama. Instead,
the French dramatist has them grow from children to young
women the same age and size as Electre.[18] Maintaining, as
always, their role as censurers of murder, they express their
disapproval in a novel way. They appear to Oreste before he
commits his crime and offer him, in exchange for ignoring the
urgings of his sister, the magnificence of a royal life and that

peace and contentment for which he longs, a peace like that which the Greek spirits help bring about. Taking on the roles of the other characters in the drama, they play out scenes in a parody of action and thus provide an ironic choral comment. They are generally saucy and impudent and they delight in mimicking Electre. One instance occurs when Electre, suddenly aware of the sacrifice she is asking of her brother, begs his forgiveness. One of the Eumenides comments, "I am depriving you of your life and I beg your pardon." (72) When she calls for her brother and she would go to him, they physically bar her way. Taking their actions into account, their method may be said to be preventative rather than punitive. Only at the end of the play, when Oreste has murdered, do they turn to pursuing him, and at this point the significance of the form they have assumed becomes immediately clear. They have transformed themselves into images of Electre so that Oreste will be pursued by the specter of the woman who drove him to commit the crime for which he is being punished. Driven to madness or suicide, he will end by cursing his sister. Such is the form of torment these Furies have devised for Agamemnon's son.

In addition to the major alterations that distinguish Giraudoux's treatment of the myth, one is struck by the excellence of his style. This greatest of all contemporary French dramatists writes a prose that is rich in poetic devices. Originality in language and imagery produces startling results. A vivid description of Agamemnon's murder — coming, effectively, immediately before the account of Oreste's murder of Egisthe and Clytemnestre — reveals that one witness remains to the first event to trap the guilty pair. When Egisthe struck the prostrate Agamemnon, his sword cut so deeply that it split the marble. The Beggar who narrates the tale reveals that he found out about the crime from the cracked tile.

A character who is borrowed from legend and transformed via Giraudoux's alchemy is the Gardener. A gentle and noble man who respects Electre, he steps aside during a brief interlude between the acts to perform the same function as the Chorus in Anouilh's *Antigone*. He offers some views on tragedy.

His humble origins may be apparent in the statement, "Kings succeed in experiments which the humble cannot perform; what they achieve is pure hatred, pure wrath." (61) In effect he is stating the most conventional theory of drama: That tragedy, reflecting the order of an aristocratic society, takes as its heroes kings rather than gardeners. The second part of the statement reveals further evidence that Giraudoux had the method of Greek tragedy in mind; we are told that tragedy is the result of purity (or extremity). The absence of moderation creates the havoc we witness towards the end of the play. Giraudoux's *Electre* opens with the arrival, amid forebodings of woe, of the disguised son of Agamemnon. It proceeds through the encounter of the prince with his sister to the moment of vengeance and ends, if not with an expected reconciliation with a benign order dispensing a new, working justice, at least on a note of peace accompanied by hope in the future of a world witnessing a new dawn. All events have occurred within twenty-four hours in the city of Argos. Upon this rigid framework Giraudoux has constructed a drama of striking freshness and lasting beauty.

*The Prodigal* (1960) by Jack Richardson is yet another variation on the woeful events in the lives of Agamemnon's children. His imagination captured by the same possibility that had occurred to the French dramatists before him, Richardson began to work with the elements of the myth to fashion a tale of youthful resistance. Unlike Giraudoux, however, Richardson makes of Orestes rather than his sister the rebel figure. Although the American dramatist is concerned with the individual's right to say no, his hero takes a cynical view of idealism. As the title of the work suggests, Orestes lacks a sense of filial devotion. Completely lacking in his makeup is any passion equal to that found in the hearts of those intense beings who dominate the works of Montherlant, Anouilh, and Giraudoux. He is incapable of progressing from a protest of his particular situation to a rebellion against his general condition, mainly because he is not disturbed by those happenings in his life that were the source of anguish for other Orestes figures. Despite the uniqueness of his experience, however, Richardson's Orestes confronts an obstacle as formidable and oppressive in its thwarting of his idea of self as that encountered by the previous rebel figures. The answer he hurls back has a recognizable ring. React differently though he may to life's challenges, Orestes has a greater kinship with the idealists than one would find him admitting.

*The Prodigal* presents the author's view of events that could have transpired between the time Agamemnon's victorious fleet is sighted approaching the Argive shore and the moment when the general-king meets his death; this last event is followed by a coda in which we have a glimpse of Orestes about to take up his role as avenger. Using known characters, Richardson studies their reactions to the dramatic situation in which they find themselves. Such reactions constitute the originality and worth of this dramatist's version of the familiar story.

The first and most significant change that Richardson makes concerns Orestes. When the returning Agamemnon walks into his palace, his grown son is there to greet him. According to the legend, Orestes was still a child at the time of his father's homecoming and death, and his years of development were spent in exile. This modern Orestes was raised in the palace at Argos, under the watchful eye of Clytemnestra and Aegisthus, and the experience has made of him a young prince who contrasts sharply with the traditional figure. The Orestes we first meet is not a man who has returned home after years of wandering abroad; he is, in fact, an individual who has been at home so long that he is quite eager to go into exile. The revolt he leads is against both the present, represented by Aegisthus, who rules as regent in Agamemnon's absence, and against the past, incarnated in the form of Agamemnon himself. Moreover, his rejection of certain conventions and attitudes of the society about him marks him as that most familiar of all modern rebels, the "beatnik." Orestes finds it difficult to communicate with his parents; likes to spend his evenings cavorting with slave girls; gets drunk regularly; sleeps through religious services; finds it difficult to be up before noon; refuses to wear conventional clothing (which, in this case, is a well-fitting suit of armor); will not take the job expected of him; generally outrages his society; and ends by attempting to carry out his greatest desire, marriage to a girl of a socially inferior status.

The modern character, it is fair to say, is the opposite of the legendary one. His tragedy is that he will be transformed, at the play's end, into the Orestes which everyone expects to meet when the curtain rises. For that legendary character is a hero — striking for all time and for all people a heroic pose — and he acts on behalf of another hero. Both the latter and the former are courageous men whose histories relate daring exploits and great deeds. Richardson's Orestes may be said to be an antihero. He protests against heroic action and argues for non-commitment. His struggle is against that traditional image the audience has in mind when it hears his name. It is a struggle to preserve his true self as opposed to his legendary self.

Because the mythological hero acts on behalf of his father, an action the modern Orestes disdains to perform, the dramatist must alter the relationship between the young prince and Agamemnon. Far from remembering him as the leader of the great expedition that set off for Troy, Orestes recalls that "he set off to mutilate Trojans." [19] When Penelope, the governess in Agamemnon's household, chides the prince for being unconcerned about the noble traditions and laws his father established, he lashes out brutally:

> I was brought stories of my father's past epic accomplishments.
> I was told how he, acting under the indubitable and humane
> principle that the seas should be free and orderly, took it upon
> himself to clear the Mediterranean of pirates, and how nearly
> a thousand of our citizens sank, as immortal heroes, of course,
> to its bottom putting this principle into effect. Was it not also
> related to me, in great detail by yourself, Penelope, how, when
> he heard a small island, I forget the name, was being ruled by
> a petty tyrant with unsavory whims, he set off to bring them

a more liberal and morally antiseptic government? I won't bother you with what principles he used there — they seemed rather muddled when I heard them the first time — but you must know their worth since a good five thousand lives were paid for them. (7)

From his father he has learned to play a game: setting the female slaves free and, after being suitably rewarded, locking them up again. Such a game, he says wryly, is called "history." Although Penelope rejoices at the thought that Agamemnon will bring with him "the old ways" when he returns, Orestes shudders at the thought, for a copybook he possesses is filled with some of his father's incisive sayings.

A most original scene in this treatment of the American author's shows the prodigal son confronting his father. According to the legend, such a meeting never occurred. The meeting is crucial in that it points up Orestes' particular grievance against his father. He is disturbed by the fact that everyone seems to cherish an illusion of the hero-king which conflicts with what he considers to be his true image. His remarks to the adoring Electra are typical. During one of the many moments when she sings the praises of her father, Orestes bursts out, in great exasperation, "Oh, if you only remembered Agamemnon as he was and not as the stories make him." (11) When Electra remembers fondly that her father would brush the flies from her face as she slept, her brother informs her that he enjoyed feeding those flies to his pet lizards. During his first encounter with Agamemnon, Orestes does his best to be civil, but it is not long before his feelings show themselves. The scene is interesting in that aside from demonstrating a novel antagonism between Agamemnon and the son he greets, we are given a view of the familial side of Agamemnon's nature. As he enters the palace he has not seen for years, he thinks of his wife and children:

> I want them now more than peace itself. I want them about me in the evenings. I would advise Orestes on women, scold Electra when she loves, or thinks she loves, some young boy I don't approve of, and, with my wife, I would argue about

petty household things and sue for forgiveness of my temper at night. (36)

Agamemnon protests that his work is done and he wants to sit by his hearth and become an idle king and doting father. However, the truth is that, like Tennyson's Ulysses, Agamemnon keeps his eye fixed on the margin of "that untravell'd world" that forever fades as he moves. The world that Richardson's character wants to explore is the one he has returned to. He is an idealist who eventually confesses that his dream, like that of Giraudoux's Egisthe, is to build a new Argos. Having set for his people examples of heroic action in the past, he begins to dream of the future and what he might accomplish if he set himself the task of working for the fulfillment of his vision. His son seems to detect this in their first encounter, and as the conqueror of Troy beams down on the underweight prince,[20] Orestes speaks what is on his mind:

> Oh, I'm tired of this farce. Who is this man leaning on a staff and calling me his son? Agamemnon, my father? What does he want here? His place is on pedestals and at the head of inspired armies. No, King of Argos, it is rather late to clasp me by the arm and call me son. It is embarrassing. (40)

Agamemnon reacts to the above with complete bewilderment, as might any father of an adolescent son: "But why should he behave in such a way?" (40)

The problem is that Orestes revolts against the idealized conception all hold of Agamemnon. In like fashion, he rebels against idealism in general and the king's brand in particular because it requires him to participate in action. Unlike Giraudoux, for whom the myth yielded a tale of tragic idealism, Richardson sees the hero as a practical individual who cannot understand the dreams of the idealists about him. Agamemnon is totally unable to understand his son, a fact that is demonstrated in a second encounter, a debate scene which is one of three in the play. Against the king's repeated pleas that he needs his aid, Orestes hurls insults; the young man tells the older man that he considers him "nothing other than an interesting but dangerous antique which still thinks it is, in some way, functional." (74) To Agamemnon's statement that the prince speaks from the vantage point of an age forged and polished by the methods of the past, an age which he helped create, Orestes replies that the creation is not yet complete and "what you offer is an unending chaos which makes improvement and justice sound suspiciously like destruction and rape." (77)

The conflict between Agamemnon and Aegisthus, who meet and greet each other with diplomatic aplomb in this play, is also dependent for its origin upon the idealist views held by the king. Rather than attempting to raise man to his greatest good, as Agamemnon wishes, Aegisthus has a different theory of governing. Aegisthus' method is to establish limits beyond which no man can go. Happiness, he believes, is created by eliminating the word "importance" from the people's vocabulary. Like Giraudoux's Egisthe, Anouilh's Créon, and Pasiphaé's society, the technique of Richardson's Aegisthus, a poet turned regent, is to eliminate everything that tends to make one individual more significant than another. It is the technique of leveling all to one common, apathetic mass. Aegisthus explains how this is accomplished:

> Into this miserable situation I came and denounced this self-styled human perfection. With my poetry I removed the word "importance" from the people's vocabulary merely by singing the absurdity, and hence equality, of all life centered about man. I told the consumptive shepherd, in simple, masculine rhymes, of course, that the martialing of sheep was as useful as the martialing of men and empires. I sang the praises of the immediate and trivial; the next rug to be woven, the next net of fish, the coming harvest, the birth of cross-eyed children. With my poetry I leveled all, and for those whose temperaments were not suited to lyrical medium I brought a religion which confirmed my more melodic truths. (19)

Like Anouilh's Créon, who admits that even he is nameless, Aegisthus includes himself in the leveling process.

In developing the character of Aegisthus and creating a motive for his murder of Agamemnon, the playwright has developed the suggestion in the myth that Aegisthus was politically ambitious rather than the idea that he was bent on avenging his father's death or the notion that he was in love with Clytemnestra. This latter motive is mentioned but discounted by the usurper himself. Aegisthus tells a surprised Agamemnon, "Whether or not you were in accord with wife and child interested me only accidentally and only as an individual. It is as a ruler that I now wish to speak." (49) And speak he does. He is very articulate as he notes for us the difference in his philosophy of kingship and that of the true ruler:

> You love man for what he might be, I for what he is. You glory in his potential, to use your own phrase; I sympathize with his existence as it is now and always will be. You cry for the heroic; I have tears of verse for the week. You give him marble principles to live by; I give him imagined reasons to live. You want him to create justice and control life; I teach him to accept the fortuitous and relish obedience. In short, you have seen man as a cause — a noble sight, no doubt of it — but it is now time to look at him unadorned and naked. (54-5)

In the interests of his cause, Aegisthus kills Agamemnon, for he knows that the king has decided to oppose him actively and wrest the power from him.

When Aegisthus discounts love as his motive, one is persuaded that he is sincere, for an earlier scene with Clytemnestra has revealed that the queen is something of a coquette (she regards him as an object on which to demonstrate the arts of love she has perfected while "practicing" on Agamemnon), and Aegisthus has to force a jealous tone. Orestes is passive about their relationship, as he is of everything else, and his conflict with his mother results not so much from her liaison with the regent (although there is a suggestion that Orestes is irritated by the sight of them together) but from the lack of understanding that exists between a rebellious son and his uncomprehending mother. Orestes protests that Clytemnestra insults his intellect when she claims that he does not understand her. Perhaps one of the reasons why Orestes tolerates his mother is that he knows that Clytemnestra's grievance against his father is similar to his own. Although the queen refers briefly to Iphigenia's death (as does Orestes), the real reason for her hatred of her husband is the fact that their temperaments are not compatible. Admitting freely that she has taken a lover, she explains to Agamemnon — who is extremely tolerant of the whole matter — that she cannot share his dreams. Where he likes to stand on mountain peaks, she does not, for the clear air at such heights causes her to become dizzy. The most original aspect of Clytemnestra is her extreme reluctance to participate in the murder of her husband; Aegisthus must force her to assist him. Her motive is novel. She fears that if Aegisthus strikes, her name will be remembered in derision, for she will be marked as a faithless woman. What she fears is the justice that eventually condemns her, that of society. When Aegisthus refuses to relent, she tells Orestes, "We shall all be judged. . . . For this day we will be tried, I know it." (88)

The gods that look down upon the regent's city aid Aegisthus in his crusade to reduce men to the point where they are mere trivialities. Aegisthus reveals that the gods — proud and scornful — remain eager to answer man's questions with an unfathomable blow of anger. Furthermore one man can desire little from another, for the gods have first choice on all that is of significant value. It is no wonder that Orestes notes, "I do as little commerce with the gods as possible these days." (14) As conflicts between characters are caused by different ways of thinking, so Orestes opposes Aegisthus because he cannot accept his views any more than he can accept those of his father:

> Between Aegisthus' creeping, crawling, microscopic figure who's buffeted by the gods and happy to be so, and my father's fumbling giant of the future who steps in everybody's garden and on everybody's toes with good intentions, the only choice is anger or laughter. I've taken the second. (68)

Orestes is not an angry young man. Such an attitude would reveal more passion than he is willing to display. Rather, his statement, "I wish my freedom to be indolent, unobtrusive, and uninvolved," (17) reveals that he is the opposite of a character like Sartre's Oreste or those figures we have discussed in this chapter who are willing to take the gravest risks, suffering even the penalty of death, in the interests of their beliefs. A very passive rebel, Orestes wants only to sit back and laugh. When Aegisthus begins to fear that he may be a threat and orders him, like Hamlet's uncle, to get out of the country (on a flimsy pretext), Orestes is overjoyed at the prospect of a well-financed and leisurely voyage.

The prince is present, however, when Aegisthus strikes and kills Agamemnon. In a scene that is unique in the many versions of the tale we have discussed, Orestes stands outside the room and listens to his father's cries as he is struck. At Electra's hysterical insistence that he pick up and use the sword the murderer drops after he has accomplished his deed, Orestes shouts, "No! Let it rest! Let it rot and crumble where it is." (95) Orestes is tired of murder and longs only for peace. Dissatisfied with his life in Argos, opposing both factions at court, he is alone in his passive protest.

He has been unable to convince even the sister who adores him to share his view of Agamemnon. Electra cherishes an illusion of her father which Orestes attributes to a childish incapacity to comprehend reality. Her attachment to her father remains strong after his death and, in contrast to her brother, she is close to her legendary counterpart. When Aegisthus orders her marriage (to a priest, this time), she agrees to the match out of a desire to punish and humiliate herself as an act of devotion to the memory of the dead king.

Orestes is similarly alone in the joy he seeks. Termed a "solitary quester" by Aegisthus, he wants only to go off to a strange land and live out his life in contented oblivion. The land he dreams of is not the never-never land which grips the imagination of the previously discussed heroines; hardly so, for it is Athens. However, in seeking to marry the daughter of a lowly fisherman, Orestes hopes to lose his identity. The influence of Giraudoux's *Electre*, noticeable at several points throughout this work (as, for example, in the repartee between Orestes and the other characters), is particularly keen in this portrait of an Orestes who longs for the quiet life. The Athens of his dreams, in fact, corresponds to the Thessaly of Giraudoux's Oreste, who rhapsodizes about flower-thatched cottages. The hero's reluctance to murder in vengeance is shared by the Orestes of the American play.

Nevertheless, despite his reluctance, Orestes will become involved, although not for the usual reason. To begin with, he does nothing to prevent his father's murder because he knows it is unavoidable. The author does not suggest that Fate is at work, for the gods have been represented as being generally unconcerned with man's activities.

Cassandra, the prophetess of the Greeks, who perceives divine forces at work, is a rather unreliable forecaster in this play. Depicted as being "small, round, and comical-looking," she is more in touch with earth than with Olympus. Her first comment, when she enters with Agamemnon, is to complain of the odor in the herring boat, which carried them ashore. To Agamemnon's reproach that as a prophetess she should have known that the wind would fail them, she parries with the announcement that she will not stoop to forecasting the weather. Rather than perceiving divine intentions, her talent is for analyzing human nature. When Agamemnon announces that he wishes for nothing more than a quiet existence before his hearth, Cassandra asks perceptively, "Can the conqueror of Troy rest?" (36) When the king goes to meet Aegisthus, with the knowledge that he will be murdered by the regent and the soldiers who have rallied around him, Cassandra ignores her own prophecy and tries to dissuade him from rash action. But Agamemnon is determined, of his own will, to die. To Orestes he comments, "I do not need her prophecy, I have my own and the living pleasure of seeing it, in part, fulfilled." (84)

Agamemnon knows that his death is the only means of forcing his son to action, and he goes to meet it in a sacrificial

frame of mind. Despite Orestes' explicit and repeated protests
that such a death will have no power over him, Agamemnon
knows the way of the world. He describes the process whereby
Orestes, despite himself, will become involved:

> You will no longer be the prince who laughs and stands aside,
> but the son who has not avenged his father's death. Wherever
> you go, you will be noticed and the world will argue and
> await your decision. You will be drawn into the current, and
> if you struggle back toward your peaceful shore shadows will
> be there to strike at your hands and force you out again into
> the center flow. You will amuse no one, for a man who bears
> the guilt of his father's death can make few people laugh.
> The world will begin to ask questions of you, Orestes, and will
> demand answers. And soon you will ask them yourself, and
> like the world you will be dissatisfied with tolerant, reasonable
> excuses. (80)

Society, then, and not any oracle will oblige him to become the
avenger. Nevertheless, the experience of the hero of the American drama is close to that of the Greek hero, for, as in the original myth, Agamemnon's murder will cause a radical change in
his life. It will cause him great personal anguish. He shares with
the hero of the original tale the fact that the source of his suffering is the necessity to fulfill an undesired obligation. However
the twist that Richardson has given to the myth involves the
nature of that necessity. Where in the Greek tale it is a divine
one, here, it is a human and social one.

The justice that prevails at the end of this play is that "dramatic justice" demanded by the majority in the audience. With
her usual perception, Cassandra (who has not been killed along
with Agamemnon but has sought out Orestes in Athens, where
he has been living since the murder on a pension provided by
Aegisthus) tell him that the majority — by which we may understand "society" — dictates the plot. It is expected of him, just
as it is expected of the hero of a grand tragedy, that he will
murder. Orestes can ignore their demands no longer. Members
of that social majority have begun to intrude upon his peaceful
life at Athens. The faithful Pylades, fulfilling like his Greek

counterpart the role of trusted friend and companion in exile, has fallen prey to the social order and has broken faith with him. The priests of Athens, judging Orestes as guilty as Aegisthus for not avenging the crime, have refused to give their consent to his marriage. Consulting the oracle, they received the pronouncement that "the Orestes known to the gods is not yet born." (102)

Orestes loses his struggle against illusions (or ideals, which for him are one and the same) and against the past. Realizing that society has defeated him, he comments bitterly, "The world demands that we inherit the pretensions of our fathers, that we go on killing in the name of ancient illusions about ourselves, that we assume the right to punish, order, and invent philosophies to make our worst moments seem inspired. Who am I to contradict all this any longer?" (109) Orestes has not been allowed to fulfill himself. Thinking of the peaceful Athenian land he must leave, he sadly looks upon his return to his native land as his "exile."

The examples of revolt we have examined have been protests against a reality the characters have found to be intolerable. The nature of that reality has differed somewhat in each case, but in each case it has been so unacceptable as to cause great suffering. The rebel is close to the type defined by Albert Camus. Although his revolt is not primarily metaphysical, he has lost his faith in a cosmic order and in a creating and benevolent god. Consequently, in the absence of universal values, he turns inward and creates his own. Although he is disturbed at the thought of death (Richardson's Orestes notes that his father's death upsets him "because it confirms my worst suspicions about this world"), he nonetheless prefers death or oblivion to a life of subjection to a force which is bent on denying him his rights. His revolt is primarily to affirm the individual as the basis of ultimate reality, the individual as the source of all authority, worth, and dignity.

As he struggles against one order, however, the rebel we have discussed offers no alternative existence. He has no ordered system of values to affirm; indeed that would defeat his own purposes, for the essence of his argument lies in individual freedom, and he avoids substituting one tyranny for another. At best he can dream only of some vague, mythical land where he can live apart from those from whom he is already alienated by the extremity of his views. When he insists on affirming his principles against all objections, he often causes great grief and destruction. The various authors, refraining from any moral judgments, simply treat the subject of moral conduct.

What the audience views is the revolt as it occurs. Little attempt is made to describe the origin of such an attitude. The suggestion appears to be that there is something within the individual's nature, difficult even for him to detect, that creates the friction. The Orestes of *The Prodigal* seems to state the case well: "Stop prompting me into a logical outline of my attitude. Differences A, B, and C, met by counterobjections 1, 2, and 3. It is nothing so finely ordered, I assure you." (76) The Chorus in Anouilh's *Antigone* states the thought another way, "It is finished. Antigone is calm now, spent by a fever the nature of which we shall never know."

## ✳ NOTES

[1] Henry de Montherlant, *Pasiphaé* in *Théâtre de Montherlant* (Paris: Gallimard, 1954). These notes are from the author's preface to the play (pp. 104–6). All subsequent page references to this edition will be given immediately after the quotation.

[2] Michel Mohrt, *Montherlant "homme libre"* (Paris: Gallimard, 1943), pp. 212–13. (The sentence quoted is from Montherlant's *Service inutile*.)

[3] Albert Camus, *L'Homme révolté* in *Oeuvres complètes* (Paris: Gallimard, 1962), p. 157.

[4] Jean Anouilh, *Antigone* in *Nouvelles pièces noires* (Paris: Table Ronde, 1958), p. 178. All subsequent page references to this edition will be given immediately after the quotation.

[5] Here, the guard is concerned about himself. In an early scene Antigone's nurse serves to add a similar human and familiar note with her concern for her young charge.

[6] Leonard Cabell Pronko, *The World of Jean Anouilh* (Berkeley and Los Angeles: University of California Press, 1961), pp. 26–7.

[7] Robert F. Coheen, *The Imagery of Sophocles' Antigone* (Princeton: Princeton University Press, 1951), p. 22.

[8] Pronko, *op. cit.*, p. 203.

[9] H. D. F. Kitto, *Greek Tragedy : A Literary Study* (New York: Doubleday & Co., Inc., 1954), pp. 133–34.

[10] Pronko, *op. cit.*, pp. 65–6.

[11] Camus, *op. cit.*, p. 232.

[12] Jean Giraudoux, *Electre* in *Théâtre* p. V. III (Paris: Bernard Grasset, 1959), p. 23. All subsequent page references to this edition will be given immediately after the quotation.

[13] The term in French is *"se déclarer,"* and Hans Sørensen has explained its full meaning. He notes, " *'se déclarer'* is not used in the usual sense of 'to make oneself known' or 'to reveal one's feelings.' Giraudoux took the liberty of extending the meaning of the term to signify, within his text, 'to realize one's destiny and to act in consequence.' " The preceding explanation is found in Hans Sørensen, *le Théâtre de Jean Giraudoux* in *Acta Jutlandica: Aarsskrift for Aarhus Universitet #22*, Supplementary Humanistic Series #35 (Copenhagen: Ejnar Munksgard, 1950), p. 117.

[14] Donald Inskip, *Jean Giraudoux, The Making of a Dramatist* (London: Oxford University Press, 1958), p. 88.

[15] *Ibid.*, p. 89.

[16] Many of the ambiguities in Giraudoux's drama are deliberate. He delights, for instance, in paradoxical and confusing statements, the meanings of which become clear at a later point. In this, too, he anticipates the method of Eliot.

[17] Marianne Mercier-Campiche, *Le Théâtre de Giraudoux et la condition humaine* (Paris: Domat, 1954), p. 228.

[18] It has been pointed out that Giraudoux must have remembered that the Greeks occasionally represented them as little girls. See Laurent Lesage, *Jean Giraudoux, His Life and His Works* (University Park: Pennsylvania State University Press, 1959), p. 189. Interestingly enough, Giraudoux's Gardener refers to them as *"des mouches."* (10)

[19] Jack Richardson, *The Prodigal* (New York: E. P. Dutton & Co., Inc., 1960), p. 7. All subsequent page references to this edition will be given immediately after the quotation.

[20] In a number of references Richardson establishes the fact that Orestes is of slight physical build. The intention is to convey further the notion that Orestes is far removed from a traditional hero.

# ※ IV

## ※ Political and Social Themes

For one of his most celebrated plays, *La Guerre de Troie n'aura pas lieu* (1935), Jean Giraudoux made use of the legend dealing with the events of the Trojan War. The subject was one to which the diplomat-dramatist was drawn because it afforded him the opportunity to express, in artistic terms, his reflections on that upheaval which periodically plagues the most civilized of nations, war, and to make an urgent though futile plea for the prevention of the holocaust of the Second World War, which he foresaw. The Trojan War, however limited its scope in actual history, presents an image of war universal enough to represent any conflict in any age, regardless of scope or duration. Its history, depicted in one of the great epic poems of Western civilization, is a history of the destruction of one civilized people by another. Troy may well be Hiroshima; the wooden horse is an early sample of man's ingenuity to produce varying means of annihilating his fellow men, of which the most devastating would appear to have been developed in the twentieth century. Jean Giraudoux was never to know of the atom bomb, having died in Paris shortly before the end of the war he had been so desirous of seeing averted; but he knew of the utter destruction which all wars bring. And the ancient Greeks

139

knew of such destruction. The chaos that reigned in Troy after Agamemnon's forces had gotten the upper hand—the murder of innocent children, the permanent separation of loving husbands and wives — has been repeated in modern times. Regardless of the means by which it is brought about, death has only one face. And the resulting grief is the same for all. If we may be detected changing color and dissolving into tears at the account of Hecuba and her despair at Pyrrhus' "malicious sport" with Priam, it may well be that the tears are sincere ones, being the expression of a personal sorrow that is brought to mind by the image of the grieving queen.

*La Guerre de Trois n'aura pas lieu* tells the story of what occurs before the Trojan War does take place. Able to maintain dramatic tension up to the ending of the work about a hypothetical situation which the audience knows from the start to be unrealizable, Giraudoux created one of his most brilliant works. The time of the play's action parallels the years before the outbreak of World War II. The novelty of the French work is that it explores, on the eve of the event, the minds and hearts of the people whose lives are disrupted by the Trojan War, the characters' reactions being, in effect, a reflection of sentiments experienced by people in the world of 1935. It has been noted that in its depiction of the hours immediately preceding the war, the play is unique in its conception and beauty among all works written in French between 1914 and 1939 on the subject of war.[1] Giraudoux has taken the mythological characters and given them roles to play, which, while not differing essentially from the roles they play in the legend, are somewhat new and unexpected. Hector is still the leader of his people, the most valiant and heroic representative of Trojan manhood. Giraudoux's hero confesses that, like the hero of old, he has a certain feeling for battle:

> Parfois, à certains matins, on se relève du sol allégé, étonné, mué. Le corps, les armes ont un autre poids, sont d'un autre alliage. On est invulnérable. Une tendresse vous envahit, vous submerge, la variété de tendresse des batailles: on est tendre parce qu'on est impitoyable: ce doit être en effet la tendresse

des dieux. On avance vers l'ennemi lentement, presque dis-
traitement, mais tendrement. Et l'on évite aussi d'écraser le
scarabée. Et l'on chasse le moustique sans l'abattre. Jamais
l'homme n'a plus respecté la vie sur son passage . . .

Sometimes, on certain mornings, you rise from the ground feeling lighter, astonished, transformed. Your body and the armor
which you bear feel less cumbersome, as if they were made of
a different alloy. You are invulnerable. You are overwhelmed
with tenderness, submerged by it, the tenderness of battle.
You are tender because you are pitiless; you experience what
must be the tenderness of the gods. You advance towards the
enemy slowly, almost distractedly, but tenderly. You even
avoid stepping on a beetle. And you brush away a mosquito
without injuring it. Never have you had more respect for the
life which crosses your path.[2]

That virility which earned for the Homeric hero the title of
"tamer of horses" remains a part of the modern character's
makeup, but Giraudoux's Hector displays his strength in a new
way. He expends his energy attempting to prolong the peace
which has followed the last skirmish in which his people have
engaged and which precedes the war with the Greeks.

If Hector is a participant in battle, he is also an observer
of its aftermath. He has walked among his wounded soldiers
and comforted the dying. The words with which he encourages
them evoke a vision of life, as does the funeral oration he is pre-
vailed upon to make in their memory. One may wonder how
many of these speeches the dramatist may have heard himself,
for the ancient tradition survived in modern times; no doubt the
best ones repeated the theme of any great tribute to the dead:
that the living, powerless to pay adequate homage to the dead,
must turn to the demands of life. Such is the theme of Hector's
speech.

Weary of battle, the young man has, aside from an under-
standable disgust with war, an added motive for desiring peace.
He is about to become a father. The child whose fate it is one
day to be hurled from the battlements of the city of which he
is a prince is yet to be born in this modern drama. Hector's

concern for his unborn son and the joy he shares with his wife, Andromaque, at the prospect of the birth, a joy like that of any ordinary husband and wife in their situation, provide some tender domestic moments. The profoundly human traits they display have their origin, no doubt, in that scene in Homer when the great hero bids farewell to his wife and son, before rushing to the defense of the failing Trojans. There Hector had stretched out his arms to take his little boy from the nurse, but the sight of his dazzling bronze and horse-hair crested helmet frightened the child, who burst into tears and clung to the woman. Hector and his wife exchanged amused glances before the warrior removed his helmet, placed it on the ground, and took his child in his arms. It is the intimacy of that scene Giraudoux reproduces in his play.

Cassandre has predicted that the war will occur, but the skeptical Trojan princess is a direct descendant of the mythological character who was given the gift of prophecy and the curse of never being believed; her warnings are not heeded. A keen observer of human nature rather than of oracular pronouncements, Giraudoux's Cassandre (on whom Jack Richardson modeled his Cassandra) reads the hearts of those about her. She knows, for example, that Hector's motives for peace are not shared by his brother, Pâris, who, it will be recalled, brought about the poor relations between Troy and Greece by seducing Hélène, the wife of Menelaus. Giraudoux's treatment of the illicit lovers is humorous and ironic. Speaking of Pâris's claim to Hélène through Venus, to whom he had awarded the disputed golden apple, Hector remarks wryly, "That was a brilliant stroke of yours that day!" (41) The Paris-Helen-Menelaus triangle is treated as an absurdity. Menelaus is an old fool who is unaware of the extent of the flirtation carried on between his young guest and his wife in his presence. As Pâris sailed away with Hélène, Menelaus was too busy to stop them, for he was wrestling on the river bank with a crab that had gotten hold of his big toe.[3] Giraudoux's farcical treatment of the Helen-Paris affair owes its existence partly to previous versions of Paris's behavior while the guest of Menelaus. At dinner one evening, Pâris embarrassed Helen by shamelessly staring at her; heaving loud sighs; picking up her goblet and putting his mouth to that part of the rim from which she had drunk; and, in a moment of abandon, tracing the words "I love you, Helen!" in wine on the table top. All of this made Helen a little nervous because her husband happened to be standing by at the moment. However she managed to keep her composure (which testifies to her talent for handling such matters). Menelaus, as unobservant as ever, cheerfully sailed off to Crete, leaving his wife to entertain his guest.[4]

Giraudoux's Pâris is equally passionate and his Hélène equally intrigued. The French dramatist, however, presents a fuller portrait of the romantic pair, who show no concern for the consequences of their act. His Hélène is not too intelligent, but she is smart enough to know that bold glances and deep sighs are not a sign of love. They are a sign, nevertheless, of a magnetic attraction, difficult to define but as powerful a force as the devotion Andromaque has for her husband. Hélène argues that the magnetism she feels is also a kind of love: "Magnetism is a love of sorts, a passion as ancient and fruitful as that which expresses itself in tears and tenderness." (145) Hélène places the emphasis on sensual love to the neglect of spiritual love. She is incapable of sincere love for Pâris. To Andromaque's impassioned demand, "Tell me that you would kill yourself if he were to die" (143) she cannot answer in the affirmative.

Pâris, too, knows nothing of eternal love; he is not the sort of fellow to brood over a broken heart. Speaking to his older brother, Pâris describes his reaction to the end of a romance:

> La séparation d'avec une femme, fût-ce la plus aimée, comporte un agrément que je sais goûter mieux que personne. La première promenade solitaire dans les rues de la ville au sortir de la dernière étreinte, la vue du premier petit visage de couturière, tout indifférent et tout frais, après le départ de l'amante adorée au nez rougi par les pleurs, le son du premier rire de blanchisseuse ou de fruitière, après les adieux enroués

par le désespoir, constituent une jouissance à laquelle je sacri-
fie bien volontiers les autres . . . Un seul être vous manque,
et tout est repeuplé . . .

Putting an end to a romance, no matter how much you love
the woman, results in an agreeableness which I am as appreci-
ative of as anyone else. The first solitary walk you take through
town, after freeing yourself from her embrace; the sight of the
first little dressmaker, unconcerned and fresh in contrast to the
weeping and red-nosed beloved you have departed from; the
ring of the laughter of laundry girls and fruit vendors, after
the sound of desperate farewells — all constitute a joy to which
I willingly sacrifice that which I have left. You lose one person
and regain the world. (36)

Pâris knows that the cure for a broken romance is a new romance. Nevertheless, his entanglements reveal that he seeks
cures in excess of his maladies. A philanderer by nature, he
is driven by lust rather than love in forming new liaisons. He is
as egotistical as the flighty Hélène. Giraudoux's ironic handling
of the legend is most evident in his depiction of the couple over
whom the terrible war is fought. Quite diminished in stature
alongside the image of immortal lovers, Pâris and Hélène are
merely selfish beings who are totally unconcerned about the
tragic events their actions bring about. That great suffering
results from their relationship is the absurdity the French
dramatist is intent on exhibiting. The overwhelming irony of
the play is the fact that it is Pâris and his faithless paramour
who separate husbands and wives like Hector and Andromaque.

In that confrontation in which she opposes her views on
love to those of Hélène, Andromaque pleads with the Spartan
beauty that she love Pâris sincerely, for then the war that will
be fought in her name will at least be fought for a noble cause
and will seem, as a result, less devoid of sense. The refinement
and gentility of Hector's wife contrasts sharply with the coarse-
ness of Hélène. What is somewhat disturbing in this scene is
that Andromaque appears to lose some of the humanity that
was apparent in the early scenes with Hector as she begins to
plead for an ideal. She becomes more like the traditional image

that usually comes to mind when we hear her name: that of the woman who mourns eternally for her dead husband, the woman who, in Racine's *Andromaque,* drives poor Pyrrhus close to madness with her refusal to yield to his amorousness. The love Giraudoux's Andromaque believes will cast some dignity on the conflict is incapable of the task, for it is alien to the lovers who are incapable of approaching such a fine emotion; and, also, it is so fine as to be almost nonexistent in the sphere of practical reality. The individual who dies for love is one of the wonders of the universe.

Pâris and Hélène, a symbol of love throughout the ages, retain their symbolic significance in Giraudoux's drama, even though they are not in love. As such, they have the support of the other Trojan citizens who are eager to wage war, ostensibly on their behalf. The old men of the town, headed by the aged King Priam, worship the pair, for in their union they see evidence of the fact that Trojans are superior lovers. When Hector attempts to appease the Greeks by assuring them that a physical relationship never existed between Pâris and Hélène and that the young man never touched the queen (except on one occasion when, moved to a frenzy beyond endurance, he kissed her hand), the men of Troy prefer to fight the Greeks rather than endure the suggestion that one of their own is impotent.

The most vociferous of the warmongers in Troy is the poet, Demokos. In the chauvinistic leader of the Trojan senate, Giraudoux has depicted the writer who, by means of his craft, inflames the mob to action. He could be the newspaperman with his provocative slanting of the truth, the propagandist who teaches his countrymen to ridicule the customs and disregard the cultural accomplishments of the enemy nation, only because it is the enemy. He also represents, to a certain limited extent, the intellectual, the pamphleteer, who writes stirring matter that plants the seed of hatred long before the first blow is dealt. Hécube describes the progression: "And after the song comes the hymn, and after the hymn, the cantata. As soon as war is declared, the poets will be impossible to restrain. Rhyme is still the best drum." (105–6) Like all those who stoop to insults and who deny others the dignity and respect due them as human beings, the warmongers end by insulting themselves.

It is Demokos who introduces Busiris, "the greatest living expert on the rights of nations," (116) to the Trojans. Busiris knows all about international law. Fate placed him on the road through Troy at this most opportune moment — the eve of the war. Representing those hagglers who argued obscure points in the years before 1939 while the lives of millions hung in the balance, Busiris provides the legal and moral justification for an attack by the Trojans upon the Greeks. Aiming his satire at the League of Nations, Giraudoux makes of Busiris a loquacious orator who lets loose a stream of rhetoric meant to convince Hector that world opinion favors Troy, for the Greeks have been guilty of three separate breaches of international law. Furthermore, like a good student, he reenforces his points with examples drawn from the history of nations that have followed the same course presently open to Troy. In the same rhetorical tone — and without the slightest degree of embarrassment — he admits that these nations that declared war on the same Greeks who are now outside of Troy and which based their actions upon the same grounds on which he now advises the Trojans to move, were defeated. Maintaining his faith in the infallibility of his reasoning, he declares: "The annihilation of a nation does not affect to the slightest degree the superiority of its moral position." (118) At the end of each argument he merely succeeds in proving the old adage that "might makes right," which is the very opposite of what he sets out to demonstrate.

By far the most serious blunder that Busiris commits is to get so involved in arguing the finer points of law that he ignores the most immediate danger: Oiax. The Ajax of *La Guerre de Troie n'aura pas lieu* is a hot-headed individual who is climbing up towards the city, hurling provocative remarks and swearing to kill Pâris. Because it is the death of Oiax that causes the Trojan Gates of War to open at the end of the drama, Busiris' judgment that the threat the rash warrior presents "is less serious" demonstrates the blindness of those intellectuals in France and Germany who, years before 1939, were so involved in quibbling over trivialities that they did not recognize the grave danger growing in their midst. While they followed the events leading to the Munich Conference of 1938, they had looked with some amusement upon the previous actions of the man in the Reich Chancellery, whom they now began to fear. Had they been alert, they would have realized that the scene which occurred in the "Bürgerbräu Keller," in the same city of Munich some fifteen years earlier — on the anniversary of Napoleon's *coup d'état* of Brumaire — represented a major political triumph for a hot-headed ex-corporal.

Only Hector fears Oiax and the harm he can do, and he realizes the futility of following the advice Busiris offers. In an amusing series of exchanges, he persuades the visiting expert to revise his view and uncover a number of mitigating circumstances that make the Greek threats appear like overtures of love. Hector manages to stave off all violence, enduring even Oiax's manhandling of his beautiful wife, in order to be able to sit down with Ulysse, the leader of the Greeks, and discuss their differences with a view towards reaching a sane solution to the problem facing both their nations. That the problem is a great one is attested to by the fact that Iris, appearing in the sky above the heads of the two great heroes, affirms that the conflict extends to Olympus, where Aphrodite and Pallas Athene, like the citizens below them, are split in regard to their feelings about the war. Aphrodite, who claims that love is the law of the world, prohibits the separation of Pâris from Hélène, and Athene, who believes that all lovers are out of their minds, urges their separation. Zeus, the great arbiter, cannot arbitrate because he is unable to make up his mind which side to favor.

In this atmosphere of belligerent gods, Hector and Ulysse sit down, like the diplomats to come at Munich, to talk about peace. Both men talk in good faith, however, which was not the case at Munich. Hector, as we have noted previously, uses his strength, a strength of spirit now, to maintain peace; Ulysse — less wiley than his Greek counterpart — works toward the same end. As he informs Hector, he will use his cunning to settle the dispute. Older and wiser, the Greek hero feels that despite their most earnest and sincere efforts, the war will come. The two nations — and we must recall that Giraudoux has France and Germany in mind at this point — have been building up gradually, imperceptibly to the level where war begins. The scales have tipped towards Ulysse and war, for the Greeks have seen and coveted Troy's golden temples and golden wheat fields. In a justly famous passage, which is surely one of the most stirring in Giraudoux's entire theater, Ulysse gives an account of the ways of diplomacy:

A la veille de toute guerre, il est courant que deux chefs des peuples en conflit se rencontrent seuls dans quelque innocent village, sur la terrasse au bord d'un lac, dans l'angle d'un jardin. Et ils conviennent que la guerre est le pire fléau du monde, et tous deux, à suivre du regard ces reflets et ces rides sur les eaux à recevoir sur l'épaule ces pétales de magnolias, ils sont pacifiques, modestes, loyaux. Et ils s'étudient. Ils se regardent. Et, tiédis par le soleil, attendris par un vin clairet, ils ne trouvent dans le visage d'en face aucun trait qui justifie la haine, aucun trait qui n'appelle l'amour humain, et rien d'incompatible non plus dans leurs langages, dans leur façon de se gratter le nez ou de boire. Et ils sont vraiment combles de paix, de désirs de paix. Et ils se quittent en se serrant les mains, en se sentant des frères. Et ils se retournent de leur calèche pour se sourire . . . Et le lendemain pourtant éclate la guerre. . . .

On the eve of every war it is customary for two leaders of the conflicting nations to meet privately at some innocent village, on a terrace in the corner of a garden overlooking a lake. And they agree that war is the worst scourge in the world; and both of them, watching their reflections and the ripples in the water, the magnolia petals falling to their shoulders, are peaceful, modest, and straightforward. They study one another. They look into one another's eyes. And, warmed by the sun, mellowed by the claret, each can find nothing in the other man's face to justify hatred, nothing which does not evoke love for mankind, and nothing incompatible any more in their languages, in their way of scratching their nose or in their drinking. And they are truly filled with peace. And they take leave of one another shaking hands, feeling like brothers. And they turn to smile as they drive away. And the next day the war breaks out. (189–2)

The diplomats of the world can merely talk of peace in our time; they cannot guarantee it, no matter how many treaties they wave in the face of a dormant Destiny. For Fate preserves hostages — a woman like Hélène, a small village, an unimportant piece of this earth — and uses it in its own time to create its own havoc. Its cruelty is that it strikes when one has just begun to enjoy a little peace. Fate hounds the efforts of diplomats — mild-mannered individuals who, over a glass of good wine, try to capture the elusive ideal which is the brotherhood of man — and thwarts them in their aims.

Hector and Ulysse look into each other's eyes and decide in favor of peace. However, as Ulysse predicts, someone unimportant brings on the terror. The poet Demokos protests the return of Hélène to the Greeks and would chant his war song. To prevent his doing so, Hector strikes him, thus committing his only violent action, a violence, ironically, committed in the name of peace. Not to be denied the sight of war, Demokos — with his dying breath — accuses Oiax of mortally wounding him. The insignificant incident becomes an international one and an immediate cause. In reprisal, the Trojans kill Oiax, and the war is on. After all the momentous issues have been weighed, all the causes examined, it is the minor incident, the rash action committed spontaneously that triggers the prepared armies. The Trojan War has begun with a lie, and lies, as Andromaque notes, breed in the climate of war: "With the advent of war, all exist in a new atmosphere of falsehood and deception. Everyone lies." (143)

The conflict that Giraudoux examines is a specific one in history, and as he writes he has in mind a specific country, a specific treaty, a specific conference. Nevertheless, the truths he affirms — the blessedness of peace, the hell which is war — are eternal ones, which emerge from the particular situation. So in the end it is not the individual speech or law that is important but the total experience which involves mankind.

The artist's particular genius in reflecting the shadow of

the future in the midst of the present is apparent in another play dealing with the same period of history as *La Guerre de Trois n'aura pas lieu*. In *Icaro* (1930), Lauro DeBosis, the Italian writer, provided an earlier example of the way in which mythological material can be used to interpret the course of contemporary political happenings. As Giraudoux was disturbed by the ominous developments in Europe prior to World War II and fearful for the tranquillity of his country, so DeBosis was unhappy about the fascist regime in power at the time in Italy. Like the French dramatist, DeBosis anticipated a period of great national suffering. He was conscious, too, of the failure of the man of intellect to alter the stream of events significantly. Seeking to arouse his countrymen to preventative and heroic action, he turned to the tale of Icarus, the ancient account of man's conquest of the skies, for a hero who could serve as a model for his countrymen. Given less to despair than Giraudoux, DeBosis illustrates in *Icaro* not the inevitability of doom but the capacity of man to accomplish the impossible.

One of the most important changes DeBosis wrought was to end his drama before that moment when Icarus, reckless of his new-found powers, soared higher and higher until the rays of the sun melted the wax fastenings of his eagle-feather wings and he plunged into the sea. When we first encounter the hero of *Icaro*, he is very much earthbound, a prisoner on Crete. In so presenting him, DeBosis recollects earlier events in the legend. The father of Icarus, Daedalus, lived in exile on Crete. He originally came from Athens and was the greatest artist of his day, a renowned architect, sculptor, and inventor.

Before going into exile Daedalus' young nephew had been apprenticed to him, and under his direction, the boy's skill had grown to the point where it surpassed his own; Daedalus became so jealous at this development that he promptly put an end to the rivalry by killing his pupil. Tried by the Athenian court of law and found guilty, he fled his native city and eventually took refuge on Crete. The ruler, Minos, welcomed him, for he had need of his skill. Daedalus constructed for him the labyrinth that confined the Cretan monster, the Minotaur.

Eventually, however, he lost favor with Minos, who imprisoned him. Longing for freedom, Daedalus wished to return home. He knew that escape by land or sea was closed to him, but the sky above was open. Using his abundant talent and ingenuity, he set about fashioning huge wings for his son and himself, as a means of effecting his escape. Before beginning their flight, Daedalus cautioned the boy not to approach too close to the sun. All went well until Icarus attempted to defy the heavens.

In a letter of about 1931, DeBosis gave some indication of his purpose in making use of the Greek myth:

> For some time I have wished to write a tragedy in verse glorifying the *élan vital* in a most heroic and personal form. The myth of Icarus is that which incorporates, more than any other, the spirit of our time. Also, it has never before been made the subject of a tragedy.[5]

In the same letter he tells of hearing of a French sonnet by the sixteenth-century poet Philippe Desportes,[6] which contains the lines,

> Icare . . . le jeune audacieux,
> Qui pour voler au ciel eut assez de courage.

> Icarus . . . the audacious young man
> Who had the great courage to fly through the skies.

DeBosis does not identify, in his letter, the force he sees opposing his Icaro, but a knowledge of his political beliefs and the facts of his life indicate one possibility, for the young poet was a militant antifascist. While lecturing at Harvard in 1926, he formulated his views, and the first indication of his disillusionment with fascism (he had previously followed with sympathy the first phase of the fascist movement) came in 1927 with the publication of his translation of Sophocles' *Antigone*. He sees Antigone as a fighter for freedom struggling against an oppressive and fascistic Creon. (In 1929, a year before its publication, his *Icaro* won a prize for poetry in Amsterdam.)

The message of the drama, masked by the myth, was not sufficiently clear to his countrymen. DeBosis had to try something bolder. Writing a number of leaflets to present his views on the danger of fascism and pleading for a conservative party, loyal to the throne and cooperating with the Vatican, which would assure personal rights and political freedom, he hit on a plan to deliver his message to the Italian people. All means of access to the country having been closed to him (his mother and friends who had aided him previously had been imprisoned), he had — like Daedalus — one last avenue open to him — the sky. He learned how to fly, purchased an airplane (which he appropriately named Pegasus) and, on the afternoon of October 3, 1931, he took off alone from Marignan, near Marseille, and headed for Rome. He reached Rome at approximately eight o'clock in the evening. Coming from a height of six thousand feet to within a few thousand feet or less of the ground, he succeeded in dropping some 400,000 leaflets over the heart of the city. The messages fluttered into the laps of spectators at an open-air cinema theater and fell into the most crowded streets. After some twenty minutes, eluding the pursuing enemy planes, he disappeared into the sky, never to return. Two years after his triumph at Amsterdam and shortly before the end of the year in which he wrote that he had wished to glorify the *élan vital*, the thirty-year-old poet was dead.

The drama he wrote is prophetic, but not strangely so, for apparently the idea of a bold venture such as that undertaken by Daedalus and Icarus had been brewing in the author's mind for some time. An examination of his work reveals the significance of the mythological hero's bold journey and helps explain the point of the flight taken by DeBosis.

The setting of the play's action is Cnossos, the capital of Crete. Icaro and his father, Dedalo, are living under oppression. The tyrant Minosse is, like his legendary counterpart, absolute ruler of the island kingdom. The tyranny the modern character exhibits is new, however. It is the tyranny practiced by dictators. He seeks to dominate men's minds, as well as their bodies.

Feigning brotherly love, he pretends to plead for Dedalo's services, though in truth he is demanding them:

> Dedalo, molto t'è concesso dire; se il corpo hai schiavo, l'anima hai divina; ma ingiusto sei con il tuo re. Non forse t'ho avuto in conto di fratello? e Creta non t'accolse da madre a non t'onora forse ella piu la tua ingrata Atene? Misera è la tua patria, aspra e selvaggia, me il regno di Minosse si distende vasto e opulento sovra tutti i mari. E più grande sarà: le mie trecento navi con ansia scuotono gli ormeggi e tra sei lune io salperò, le rosse prore rivolte verso l'Asia immensa. Dedalo, e tu de la titania impresa sarai la mente. Tu col genio ed io col mio potere, a sarà nostro il mondo.

> Daedalus, this much may be said; if your body is enslaved, your soul is divine. But you are unjust with your king. Have I not always treated you as a brother? Has not Crete received you lovingly, and does she not honor you? Perhaps more than your ungrateful Athens? Your land is mean, crude, and untamed; but the kingdom of Minos stretches in vastness and richness beyond the seas. And it will be greater still: my three hundred ships eagerly pull at their moorings. And within six months I will weigh anchor, the red prows of my vessels turned towards the huge expanse of Asia. And you, Daedalus, shall mastermind this enormous undertaking. With your genius and my might, we shall rule the world.[7]

Minosse is not content to rule Crete; he wants to rule the world, and he is depending upon Dedalo's abilities to help him accomplish his goal. He bribes the artist with a promise he has no intention of fulfilling, "Lush Attica shall be yours." (22) In order to dominate the world, Minosse will need superior weapons and Dedalo soon provides him with one — iron. Producing a sword wrought from the new metal, the Athenian craftsman demonstrates its superiority over weapons made of inferior materials. Minosse is elated.

However, Icaro, who is standing nearby, is shocked at his father's actions. The young man had dreamt of liberating the enslaved peoples of the world with the wondrous iron sword. Dedalo shrugs off considerations about tyranny and liberty:

Tiranni e libertà passano entrambi;
crollano i regni a crollano gli Dei
Solo il pensiero vigilante avanza
e inalza un tempio, la Scienza, a fronte
di cui l'Impero de la terra è nulla.

Tyrants and liberty both expire;
Kings and gods decay
Only the vigilant intellect devises
and creates the temple, Knowledge, before
which the earthly empire crumbles. (31)

DeBosis has created two types of idealists in the mythological father and son. Dedalo is a thirsty seeker of knowledge,
but he seeks it for its own sake. He looks to the future for fulfillment, "I live amongst those who have yet to come." (31)
He has no desire to remedy the present ills of the world. In
reply to Minosse's offer to grant him anything he desires in
exchange for the gift of iron, Dedalo requests "solitude." An
isolationist at heart, Dedalo is not so very different from those
rebels we have examined in the last chapter. He seeks freedom
only so that he may be allowed to realize himself; he offers no
program for the solution of political and social problems. In the
society that DeBosis was representing, Dedalo is the intellectual
who has the power to change the world but who refuses to
commit himself to any cause.

Dedalo is a scientist and Icaro is a poet. The young man
is DeBosis himself, quite transparently so, in fact. Echoing the
thought of Percy Bysshe Shelley, with whom he had many
ties, DeBosis has Icaro reveal the function of the poet in society:

Ogni poeta è un nunzio
tra i due mondi: dal nostro eleva i cuori
a le musiche eteree, ma da quelle
trae le scintille a fecondar la nostra
fertile terra; e quel che oggi è sogno
per virtù del poeta si fa viva
forza operante, una terrena cosa;
da cui altri poeti spiccheranno
il volo un giorno, verso nuovi sogni,
che oggi non pur sfiorano la mente.

> Every poet is a messenger
> between two worlds: he puts earthly spirits
> in touch with the music of the spheres, and
> draws divine fire to spark the awakening of
> earth. And that which today is a dream
> becomes tomorrow through the genius of the poet
> a vital, energized reality—an earthly incendiary
> to enkindle the imagination of succeeding poets
> to new dreams hardly conceivable to men today. (39)

The poet moves between the spiritual world and the material world. A herald of future events, he seeks to spread the truth to all corners of the earth. He alone "lifts the veil from the hidden beauty of the world" and seeks thereby to ameliorate his society. Like Shelley, who was also involved in youthful political activity, DeBosis would affirm that "poets are the unacknowledged legislators of the world."

Icaro's program calls for him to spread the message of freedom. In a conversation with Fedra, the daughter of Minosse and Pasifae, he is called upon to defend his views. Fedra, who seems to anticipate Giraudoux's caustic commentary on jingoistic writers, inquires of Icaro if it is not true that poets are always ready to glorify war:

> Non son forse sempre
> pronti gli aedi ad esaltar le guerre?
> Non forse cantan essi per dar gloria
> a chi vince e nei secoli venturi
> far grande il nome degli eroi?

> Are not poets
> always ready to exalt war?
> Do they not sing to glorify
> conquerors and to immortalize
> the names of heroes? (54)

Icaro explains patiently that the new poets, of which he is one, have more noble dreams than those of men dying on battlefields:

Gli aedi
nuovi più grandi eroi sognano e gloria
più alta che d'uccidere sul campo
figli di madre e incendiar città.

The new poets
dream of greater heroes, of
nobler deeds than the slaughter
of men and the burning of cities. (55)

Rather, the new poets will sing of the triumph of the free and
the wise over whatever dark, low, and iniquitous force oppresses
man.

For all his talk of freedom, however, Icaro is a slave, not
so much to Minosse but to his beautiful daughter, for he is in
love with her. Moreover, he is unhappy, for he has not declared
himself and is uncertain of her feelings. The chorus of Minoan
maidens enters and, following the traditional role of the Greek
chorus, comments on the action — singing of the pangs of unrequited and inexpressible love. Summoning up the kind of
courage he is to demonstrate later on with his flight, Icaro
finally tells the princess the truth. The result is disaster. Fedra
spurns him. She tells him that she is waiting for a man who
can afford to keep her, as the saying goes, in the style to which
she is accustomed, "Fedra will love only the man who will give
her the most splendid kingdom." (38) She is the daughter of
a king, and she will wait for a king. The king she is waiting for,
following the order of the myth, is Theseus, or Teseo, who does
arrive towards the end of the drama. Icaro is crushed, and
burying his face in his hands, he weakens and sobs as the scene
ends.

DeBosis has injected a little romance into the legend for
a specific reason. Fedra, at this point, symbolizes those still to
be won over to the cause. Icaro's failure affects him deeply
and, disillusioned, he resolves on ignoring the call to heroic
action and surrounding himself with all the pleasures of the
earth. On this cue Fedra's mother enters. In this drama Pasifae
preserves her image of a passionate woman. No longer enam-

oured of the bull, she now turns her attentions to the young man. She makes, with the greatest of ease, the difficult admission that she no longer loves her spouse but loves him instead. Were she to present some reasonable explanation of how such a sad state of affairs has come about, one could look upon her with sympathy. Instead, Pasifae goes coolly on to suggest that they kill Minosse and take over the kingdom. Although he has no affection for the king, Icaro is appalled at her suggestion (DeBosis does not advocate assassination), and he rejects her.

The scene with Pasifae is significant in that it represents a way of life open to the idealist who is bound to meet with disillusionment. The temptation to lead a life of ease, rather than to continue a struggle on behalf of an elusive ideal, is particularly strong when one meets with disappointments. The introduction of a Pasifae who is scorned by Icaro also allows DeBosis to introduce the idea that Icaro's death is not an accident but a wilful act perpetrated by a vengeful and jealous god. Resentful of his treatment of her, Pasifae calls upon her father, the Sun, to destroy the young man with his fires.

The gods in DeBosis' drama are jealous ones. They are envious of Icaro, for they consider him a rival for their territory, which is the sky.

Dedalo has told his son of his latest invention, the wings made from eagle feathers, and Icaro has dreamed that the wings will liberate man. The symbolism is apparent here. The sky is the new kingdom within man's power to attain, a kingdom free of the taint of despotism. The gods are the important figures of the fascist regime. In advancing his own vision and reaching a perceptive audience, Icaro holds some power himself. During his actual flight, Fedra calls out, "Lo! He is lost among the gods." (126) Fate, the gods, and Minosse all combine to represent the oppressors, though for reasons we will next examine, Minosse separates himself from the other two.

When Minosse finds out about the wings Dedalo has constructed, he also discovers that the two men plan to use those wings to escape Crete and fly back to Athens, their plan in the original tale. Minosse reacts to the realization that his slaves

are about to free themselves in typical fashion: he orders Dedalo imprisoned and his wings burned; when Icaro comes to
his father's aid, the king orders the boy thrown into the lion's
den. At this point Fedra, who has been won over by the young
man's idealism and has come to love even the sound of his
voice, intercedes for him. (The king's astonishment that his
daughter is willing to give up the kingdom of her dreams for
the love of a humble poet provides one of the few light moments in this serious drama.) What exerts the greatest pressure
on Minosse to relent in his persecution of Icaro and his father,
however, is a happening the king takes as an omen. He hears
that an eagle has swooped down into the lion's den and carried
away one of the cubs, and the wind has showered down lilies
on the spot from which the animal was taken. Minosse concludes that Icaro belongs with the eagles rather than with the
lions and agrees to let him make the flight. In DeBosis' version
of the myth, only Icaro is allowed to fly — Dedalo must remain
on the ground — for only Icaro has the desire to spread the
message of freedom.

Minosse's conversion to Icaro's side (as well as that of
Fedra) is somewhat unconvincing and is the most serious flaw
in the work. In modernizing the legendary king of Crete, De-
Bosis had the image of the Italian king in mind. The poet
resented Victor Emmanuel's surrender to the fascist movement,
which had occurred as early as 1922 when Mussolini marched
on Rome and the king refrained from signing the proclamation
of martial law unanimously decided upon by his cabinet. De-
Bosis had built up a grievance against the ruler of his country
because he believed that the Crown, by acquiescing to Mussolini, had betrayed the constitution it had sworn to uphold. It
had allowed the covenant to be violated and had seen,
without flinching, the destruction of constitutional liberties.
One of the leaflets DeBosis dropped on Rome was addressed
to the king of Italy. Urging him to champion the cause of freedom and break with the fascists, DeBosis pleaded, "Do not
compel the Italian people to regard you as responsible for this
oppression. . . ." [8]

Minosse fears the gods above him. Along with the priests, he fears — above all — the punishment of the dread Minotaur, which is a symbol, in this drama, of the gods' vengeance. Nevertheless, he relinquishes his oppressive hold on the poet. In allowing Icaro to fly, the king is conscious of the fact that he is breaking the decree of the gods; when he relents, he orders that sacrifices be made to the deities to appease them.

DeBosis wished so greatly to see the living king won over to his cause that he forced the conversion of the character who represents him in the play. Minosse does not yield because he comes to believe in Icaro; he changes his mind because of a miracle. The happy ending to the dispute between the poet and the monarch does not arise logically from the preceding event but is imposed from without. DeBosis here displays a woeful ignorance of human nature, as well as an error in dramaturgy. Even a miracle would not have sufficed to change the Italian king.

As Icaro ascends the heavens, the Chorus breaks out into a joyful dance of triumph. They sing of hope for the future when man can live in peace and freedom, and they indict the scourge which is war.

As those who remain behind at Crete anxiously wait for news of Icaro's safety, a herald enters. He announces that an Athenian ship with black sails has been sighted approaching the shore. It is the ship bearing the seven youths for the sacrifice to the Minotaur. Fedra, who fears that the sight signals some presage, reveals that Icaro had sworn that he would liberate these youths from death. Teseo, the leader of the Athenian band, enters and announces that they have sighted and conversed with Icaro. The man flying above the ship had shouted a question to its captain, "Brother, towards which port do you sail?" Teseo replied, "Towards Death." And the prince added, "I go to die for my country within the labyrinth of Minos." (143) Teseo's disclosure that the port he is navigating towards is death reveals that he has no future. The Italian dramatist has augmented his story of Icarus with material drawn from the episode telling of Theseus' adventure at Crete.

Teseo and his little band represent the oppressed people of the world drifting slowly but inevitably towards a death-like existence. It is to these people that Icaro shouts his message:

>                              Resiste al Fato
> Questo è il messaggio d'Icaro: combatti!
> prendi la Morte pei capelli e vinci.
>
>                              Resist your destiny:
> This is Icaro's message: Fight!
> Seize Death by the hair and conquer! (147)

Icaro's message, of course, is a simplification of the call to resistance DeBosis was to drop upon the capital of his country. The death his people faced was that brought about by a regime which, as he tells the Romans in one of those leaflets, "not only corrupts your souls but destroys your substance, paralyzes the economic life of the country, squanders millions to prepare for war and hold you in submission, piles up public expenditures over which you have lost all control, and abandons the country to the rapacity of its fortune-hunting leaders." [9]

DeBosis was an optimist, as the action of his play demonstrates. The ship he chose for his hero to meet, of all those black-sailed vessels that made their way periodically to Crete, was the one that would return with the conqueror of the Minotaur aboard. Also, ignoring the fact that Theseus was saved by Ariadne, the Italian dramatist makes Icaro provide the inspiration that sees Theseus through his ordeal. DeBosis believed that Icaro could succeed.

Although Teseo describes Icaro's death, all who remain behind know that his spirit lives forever, and they praise him:

> Gloria in eterno ad Icaro ed a l'uomo!
> Gloria a chi osa!
>
> Eternal glory to Icarus and to man!
> Glory to those who dare! (156)

Icaro's flight is the free expression of a free spirit. It is the glorious expression of man's creative ability and his capacity to change the world in which he lives. If the action of both DeBosis and his hero seems rash and impulsive, an expression of a hot-headed and revolutionary temperament, requiring only the addition of some ten or so years to transform it into the most conservative and practical of spirits, at least it demonstrates a quality that never grows stale: courage. DeBosis and his hero remain forever a symbol of a type of temperament that does indeed change the world, the type described, to repeat Desportes' phrase, as *"le jeune audacieux."*

In directing their attention to the affairs of their nations, writers have been moved to illuminate social problems as well as political issues. Frequently, of course, the two are inseparable. Certainly the most crucial development in the sphere of twentieth-century world politics has been the confrontation of East and West. One writer who was sensitive to the effects of that confrontation upon the relations of human beings within the social community was the French dramatist H. R. Lenormand. Lenormand discovered that in addition to yielding material that enables us to focus on the affairs of governments, myths are valuable in aiding the artist who seeks to expose to view the interaction of individuals who fall heir to the deeds of their leaders. The tale that most suited his purpose was that of Medea and Jason. Considering the situation at the core of the myth, the French author was able to reduce it to the following: After a courtship marked by passion and violence, a couple soon discover that they hold opposing views on how to live life; such opposition transforms their passion into hate and destroys their marriage. In Lenormand's play *Asie* (1931) the theme of marital discord is given a modern social reality. The discord is viewed as the direct result of racial prejudice and of individual personality differences based upon the fact that the principal characters represent two alien cultures. The playwright remembered that the unhappy union of the Thessalyian hero and his Colchian sweetheart was one between a civilized Greek and a semi-barbaric stranger who worshipped strange gods and practiced strange customs. In that experience, that blend-

ing of two cultures followed by a most violent un-blending,
Lenormand saw an opportunity to study the marital situation
of a modern European and his Asian wife. He explores the varying pressures, from both within and without, that destroy their
happiness.

The opening action of *Asie* occurs on a Far-Eastern mail
boat. The principal characters are on board, and the first ones
we meet are an elderly gentleman, De Listrac, who has been
in the employ of the French government in Indochina for the
past thirty years, and his daughter, Aimée. They are discussing
the hero, De Mezzana, whom they have known for only four-
teen days. Aimée is visibly impressed by the tales she has heard
concerning the man she has recently met. De Mezzana is a
colonial boy, an adventurer whose exploits, which include the
domination of completely savage tribes, recall to her mind a
Livingston or a Stanley. To our mind he recalls another hero.
Possessor of "the ancient heritage of conqueror and organizer," [10]
the forty-year-old De Mezzane is a modern counterpart of the
Greek Jason. Traveling with him is his wife, an Asian princess
named Katha Naham Moun, who is the Medea of the play.
That there is something out of the ordinary about this couple,
aside from the obvious racial difference, is borne out when
De Mezzana reveals the circumstances of their courtship. For
love of the white man she was to marry, the Princess conspired,
like the legendary heroine, against her father, who was the
ruler of the kingdom of Sibang in Indochina. Recognized as
chief by two thousand warriors, the Frenchman remained to
rule and lead the people to victory for a period of eight years.
Conspired against in turn, and the object of much hatred, De
Mezzana has had to flee the country to avoid being assassinated.

When we first meet him, the hero is en route to pick up
his two children, who have been left in the care of missionaries
for the past three years; then he plans to return to France.
An ambitious man, like the legendary Jason, he has submitted
his credentials to De Listrac, a person of some influence. De
Mezzana has hopes of resuming a career in France, and the
older man looks with considerable interest upon his abilities

and background. The only factor that appears to impede the adventurer's progress is his wife. Screening the lady, as well as her husband, De Listrac has arrived at the conclusion that the Princess will have difficulty adjusting to the environment of France. Her indomitable spirit gives her away. With some embarrassment, and begging the younger man's forgiveness, the colonial administrator notes that a certain savage element in Katha's nature gives him the impression that she is capable of great crimes. De Mezzana agrees, for he reveals that he would have preferred to leave the lady behind, except for the uncomfortable certainty that had she discovered his plans she would have killed him.

The modern Jason's desire to divorce his wife is the same as that of his Greek ancestor. He is tired of a disordered existence and the violence which, in addition to the Princess' betrayal of her father, included the murder of her innocent brother. He longs to settle down to a respectable career and "a French wife" in a villa on some placid coast where he can sit on his terrace and sip a glass of good rosé rather than tea.

Lenormand has added a new theme to his version of the myth. The reference to "a French wife" provides us with a clue. A growing rift is developing between the couple based on the fact that they are members of different races. When De Mezzana thinks of the children in whom their blood is mixed, he makes the admission — strange for a father — that he has difficulty remembering their faces. He adds — and he explains all by the addition — "I cannot remember the shade of their skin." His wife, alert to this, answers him — employing an endearment that seems a bit insincere, "Like mine, Dear, only a bit lighter." However, De Mezzana insists, "A great deal lighter, I think." Not to be outdone, Katha must have the last word, "Only a little. Only a very little." (23)

The girl that the hero wants to leave his wife for is Aimée. The daughter of the powerful De Listrac, who is the counterpart of the ancient king of Corinth, she is Creusa. In physical appearance she is the opposite of the Asian princess. Tall and blonde, she exudes refinement and contrasts markedly with

Katha. Although her father used to be an influential man himself, De Mezzana's wife displays a crudeness which is alien
to the well-bred Aimée. The contrast between the two women
is a bit obvious, as is the symbolism. Katha represents Asia
and Aimée is Europe. In going from one to the other De
Mezzana is renouncing his loyalty to his life in his adopted
country and seeking the life he left behind in France. He cannot
belong to both worlds or to both women at once, for as Aimée
indicates, the man who can do that has to be something of a
genius. When the disillusioned conqueror of Sibang tells De
Listrac's daughter, "You are Europe, towards which I feel myself drawn with greater urgency each day." (38) Aimée protests, "But you are married." Nevertheless, De Mezzana re-
assures her, "I was married to the beat of war drums, by howl-
ing demons entwined in yellow silk." (39) The talk about the
tom-toms is revealing. He is telling her that a religious difference as well as a racial difference exists between him and his
wife and that the marriage lacks the validity that would make
a divorce difficult to secure. His words open up all sorts of
moral and legal aspects to the situation, which, in modern
times, have become the subject of much study. They also echo
an aspect of the ancient myth. Jason and Medea plighted their
troth before the altar of Hecate, the divinity who represents
the darkness and terrors of the night. Medea's continual worship of the dread goddess caused the friction in her marriage.

That Lenormand may have had the preceding fact in mind
may be supposed from the imagery of a passage which comes
before the one where the hero tells about his unusual marriage
ceremony. Aimée has expressed the thought, natural enough
in such a circumstance, that although De Mezzana claims that
he wants her because she inspires him with confidence and the
joy of living, he must certainly have made a similar admission
to the lady to whom he is presently wed. In reply her suitor tells
her that he made the error of mistaking infatuation for love.
He was intrigued by the exotic, the strange. Instead of searching for common interests in his future mate, he relished the
differences. Katha, like Medea and her goddess, is identified

with the mysteriousness of the night. The young De Mezzana was fascinated, and, from what we gather, the opposition to the match — coming mainly from her people — only made it the more attractive, for it then took on that appeal which attaches to anything that is forbidden. Unfortunately, the hero lives to regret his error of judgment. What seemed to him to be exotic and attractive turned into an object of hatred because of the fact that his wife's development did not parallel his own. The woman that seemed so suited to him in Sibang could not be the companion of the man he had grown into. When her husband tries to explain the change in temperament he has undergone, she can only refer to the sacrifices she has made for him in the past.

This treatment of the Medea legend is marked by a considerable number of domestic scenes in which De Mezzana and his wife are shown with their children, who have large speaking parts. It is mainly through the two boys that we discover the dissenting force that religion plays in their lives. The children had been sent away from their mother's kingdom and educated by French missionaries. The reason for the displacement was their poor health. Suggested is the rather fanciful notion that their native air did not agree with them because they were of mixed blood. Once away and under the influence of their teachers, they are baptized into the Christian faith and given the names of French saints. When she sees them again, Katha is shocked at the sight of them marching in a religious procession, and when she calls them by the names she has given them, Apaït and Saïda, they do not respond. With considerable anger, the distraught woman reaches the illogical conclusion that because their names reflect the religion of their father, the boys no longer belong to her.

The attempt to make Christians out of the boys is one example of the different forces which begin to exert an influence towards Europeanizing or Frenchifying the children, thus separating them from their mother and their mother from their father. Another pressure is that which may be termed "cultural progress." There is constant opposition throughout the drama between a civilized, progressive Europe on the one hand and a backwards, primitive Asia on the other. That counteraction is an enlarged view of the conflict that exists between Jason and Medea in the legend. In *Asie* it is most clearly manifested in the attitude of the parents towards the education of their young. The boys have inquisitive minds and are interested in learning about machines and mechanical matters, as would any boys their age. De Mezzana tries, as much as he is able, to explain to them the scientific truth they seek. Yet whatever headway he makes in that direction, his wife offsets with explanations that are based on superstition and magic. Thus one youngster announces that the ship on which they are traveling is not propelled by a machine but by a monster.

The question of the education of the children becomes a matter of contention between De Mezzana and his wife, and they begin to bicker. Perhaps thinking of the Europeans who have begun to penetrate her country. Katha charges, "You will make engineers of them, right? Frantic little men in white helmets building bridges and canals." De Mezzana snaps back, "I certainly won't make magicians of them." (45) And the battle is on!

Once in France, the children have difficulties in school. Their coloring makes them an object of curiosity and ridicule to their little classmates. Gradually the prejudices of the society to which De Mezzana belongs are revealed. The boys, the oldest one in particular, begin to react sensitively to Katha in relation to the new environment. He attempts to cheer his mother up by telling her, "It's not your fault if you are a little dark," (54) but he soon admits, displaying a maturity beyond his years, that "A white mother would be more practical for traveling." (55)

The white mother who is to take the Princess's place is Aimée, and she is not too happy about it. The portrait of Creusa in this play is a particularly warm and tender one. She is heartsick at the thought that she will be responsible for separating the children from their mother (for it is De Mezzana's plan that Katha return to her own country and leave the children to him). She feels somehow that she is an accomplice in a crime and expresses repeated concern for the Princess. Her love for De Mezzana's children is sincere, and when the father and boys are installed in their hotel near Marseille, she comes to visit them, bringing gifts for the boys that are themselves meaningful. She brings them bicycles, thus indicating that she belongs more to the mechanical, progressive world of their father than does his wife. Aimée pleads with De Mezzana that he allow Katha to remain nearby, allowing her to see the children, but he refuses on the grounds that the woman would be obsessed by the thought of the couple's happiness. He cannot tolerate the idea of the children being raised by their mother because he does not want to see them grow up as "savages."

Her husband believes that there is something evil in Katha that makes her destructive, and he is correct. That strain of irrationality that characterized the Greek princess is apparent in the modern Medea's temperament. Just as the Colchian sorceress murdered an innocent girl, so Katha vows to use any available means to destroy her rival. On the verge of hysteria, she cries out, "I will kill her! I will disfigure her. And that is one crime which I will never regret." (83) Such a sentiment goes beyond ordinary jealousy. Her attitude towards Aimée appears even more unreasonable than that of Medea towards Creusa for Aimée is portrayed as a sympathetic character who takes Katha's part at every juncture.

The modern Medea's cunning is demonstrated in a scene that parallels the meeting between the legendary character and Créon, the king of Corinth. De Listrac goes to see Katha. Fearing for the life of his daughter, he is wary of the Princess's resources and tricks. He hopes to encourage her with the news that the country to which she will return is one that is slowly emerging from "barbarism," due to the generosity of foreign investors. The reason for Katha's poor opinion of engineers becomes apparent in this scene. It is based on a deep resentment of the Europeans who have begun to invade her land. Lenormand was distressed by the abuses of French colonialism, and the myth provided him with an occasion to censure his greedy countrymen. Furthermore Jason and his followers were strangers in the land of Colchis, and their presence did little to promote domestic tranquillity. Such is the basis for the development of the imperialism theme in *Asie*, a theme foreign to the myth but which, nevertheless, suggests itself to the dramatist eager to exploit such a possibility. It can be handled, moreover, without doing any violence to the inevitable progression of events. To bring his theme to the fore, the modern dramatist makes use of the clash between Medea and Creon, her ancient enemy. Once the subject has been introduced, De Listrac proceeds to rhapsodize on the generosity of foreign investors and the great benefit to come from the influx of foreign capital in Sibang, "Do you realize what that means? Highways, commerce, railroads. In sum, it means security, progress!" Chafing at the man's references to her country as a barbaric one, Katha replies, "And a French governor in my capital; I understand." (100) Katha feigns submissiveness, for she is playing for time, as did Medea. Interestingly enough, however, the reasons she gives for her reluctance to return home are not those of the Greek heroine. Medea feared the reprisals that would come from the followers of those she wronged; Katha fears the Europeans and their culture. She fears exploitation by imperialist intruders. When De Listrac leaves, she has gained what she sought — ten additional days in the country. Her true feelings come out after Aimée's father has departed: "Ten days! Ten days from which must issue years of suffering for the race of my enemies." (102)

The Princess's last request of her husband is that she be allowed to live the last ten days with him and the children in De Mezzana's villa on the outskirts of Marseille. He agrees. As soon as they meet they begin arguing again. His wife's strategy involves getting the hero to admit that he loves his children more than Aimée, more than himself in fact. As soon as she does so, she knows that she can use the children as an effective weapon against her husband. She first makes sure of the extent of their loss to him, and then she kills them.

Katha lacks some of the weapons of the legendary heroine; she does not make use of a poisoned robe and crown of gold. Nevertheless she alters the stream of Aimée's life. Had De Mezzana chosen the girl in preference to his sons, there is no doubt that Katha would have killed her outright. That not being the case, the Asian princess chooses a similarly cruel way to avenge herself on her well-intentioned rival. She knows that by killing the children and destroying her husband she will destroy whatever life Aimée and her husband could have had together. The thought brings Katha some measure of comfort.

Katha has realized that her husband has made progress in regard to his ideas concerning the education of the boys and that they are slowly adapting to their father's society. After some moments of hesitation, she goes through with her scheme to murder the youngsters. The last act of the drama is interesting because all the motifs developed in the preceding scenes are reintroduced. After her final decision has been made, the Princess thinks of the sort of future her children will have if they remain under De Mezzana's influence:

> Non, ils ne deviendront pas les domestiques des monstres qui mangent l'espace! Ils n'inventeront pas de machines. Ils ne tireront pas de leurs cervelles ces cauchemars de roues, de griffes et d'éclairs. Je sauverai l'âme que je leur ai donnée! La chose pure et sans poids que l'homme reçoit de l'homme, je la sortirai de l'enfer des chiffres et de la vitesse!

> No, they will not become the servants of monsters who devour space. They will not invent machines. Their imaginations will not spawn the nightmare of roads, rubber stamps, and flashes. I will save the soul which I gave them! That gift, pure and free, which man receives from man. I will save them from the inferno of figures and speed! (120–1)

Her resentment against Christianity and the influence it wields as opposed to her own becomes once more apparent in the death scene itself. De Mezzana's villa is situated near a convent. From the chapel of that convent can be heard the voices of women singing a hymn of praise to the Virgin. As the children begin to fall into a deep sleep, induced by the poison their mother has given them, the sound of the singing comes to them and soothes them. As the stage directions indicate, Katha is disturbed at this: "The Princess listens, her face contorted in instinctive protest against these voices which, at the last moment, appear to frustrate her, bringing the children a peace and a liberation other than that which she has chosen for them." (144)

Finally, the Princess's sense of the imperialist exploitation of her country by the French comes once more sharply to the surface in an exchange with De Mezzana where he assures her that chiefs of industry are taking over the territory previously held by chiefs of warrior tribes. She thinks of her people, of their plight if they are to become the slaves of an industrialized society. She regards the intrusion of the mechanical world of progress as signaling an end to the free existence her people cherish. She is moved to tell her husband that men of his breed will make of Asia "a hell comparable to your own." (123)

To the Greek Medea's most violent action, Lenormand added a modern motive. Like her ancient ancestor, Katha wishes to destroy her husband. However, she differs from the classical heroine in that she has the additional desire to put an end to that part of her, perpetuated in the children, which had embraced an alien culture. She strikes out as much in hatred of her husband's world as of the man himself. With the death of the children she feels herself finally free of Europe and, in the final moments of the play, she addresses the Sun, crying, "I have regained my kingdom!" (146)

The drama has preserved none of the unities, and Lenormand has altered, quite radically, the plot structure of the tale. Nevertheless, it is apparent throughout that he is telling the story of Medea and Jason. Their experience forms the basis of the entire work. The French author's play expresses, as does the ancient tale, the bitterness of love that has turned to hate. It is a look at disillusionment, at youthful error, added to which is the gnawing pressures of a hostile society. The sorceress of Colchis and her hero who had one day sailed victoriously through the Hellespont into the Greek sea become a man and woman, fundamentally different, who cannot live with their differences. Set in modern times, the work is realistic in conception and details. Once more, the myth is brought closer to everyday reality through the use of anachronisms. Thus the children of the modern Medea talk about automatic devices, and her Jason lives in a villa with a convenient location: it is only twenty minutes by car from his office in Marseille.

Five years after Lenormand's *Asie* made its appearance at the Théâtre Antoine in Paris, Maxwell Anderson's *The Wingless Victory* (1936) was first performed at the National Theater in Washington, D.C. The American drama is another version of the Medea myth, and it explores many of the themes Lenormand took up in his play. Anderson, too, concentrates on that disorder the French dramatist observed and which, decades later, was to become a major social problem in the United States — racial prejudice. Although his heroine is modeled on the mythological figure, her experience is that of any individual who encounters the evil of bigotry. The Medea myth, with its image of a union that is doomed to failure because the individuals involved are members of different peoples and have grown apart from one another, served Anderson's purpose as it did that of Lenormand. The American playwright does not, however, search for a political cause to explain the social ills he perceives. He is content merely to expose the problem and its effects. The exploitation motif is sounded briefly; there is little suggestion that the author intends an indictment of his countrymen.

Although *Asie* and *The Wingless Victory* bear many similarities, the action of the latter work is far removed from the sad land of Indochina. Anderson's conception required a New England setting. His Jason is Nathaniel McQueston, a member of an influential shipping family of Salem in the year 1800. Just why the archetypal Jason should assume this shape becomes apparent when we consider the dramatist's procedure in adapting his source material. Lenormand creates social conflict in his drama by focusing on the abuses of colonialism. His view, a personal one, is that of a Frenchman who reacts against the policy pursued by his country in a foreign territory. Likewise Anderson, aware of the possibility of developing a social theme out of the fabric of the myth, reached back into his own nation's past for an irritant. He found it in that force which possibly, more than any other, had the deepest effect upon the national character — Puritanism. The hero of the American play experiences tragedy because he runs counter to the code of his community. The first error he commits is to profit from this sort of mischief, for he returns to his home town as master of his own vessel, loaded with the treasure of the East, and thus incurs — in the absence of the wrath of God — the wrath of Salem. The trouble begins to brew in the New England town when it is discovered that Nathaniel's cargo of imports includes goods other than spices. On board ship are two Malay women and two children, of "a faint coffee-color." One of the women is Oparre, Princess of the Celebes, who is Nathaniel's wife. The children belong to the couple, and the second woman is Toala, Oparre's maid. Maxwell Anderson takes up the story of Medea and Jason at the same point Lenormand and the Greek dramatist Euripides did, after the couple has been married some seven to ten years. Following his fling at adventure, Nathaniel, like his predecessors, longs to settle down to a peaceful life. The difficulties that the couple has in adjusting to the world of Salem — difficulties that destroy their marriage — form the substance of the American drama. Like the French dramatist, the American playwright focuses on some of the pressures which begin to gnaw at the modern Colchian princess and her lover. A major innovation of Anderson's is his creation of Nathaniel's family. He has endowed his Jason with a mother and two brothers, one of whom is a puritanical minister. The American dramatist creates a family for his hero because he wishes to demonstrate the ways of family opposition to the mixed marriage. Mrs. McQueston and the Reverend Phineas McQueston serve to provide a clue to the community fiber. Even before meeting Oparre, they form their bigoted opinion that she must be inferior because "she's a black, and worships some pagan fetish." [11] What Phineas is like is made apparent in the first moments of the drama when the minister is discovered in the process of ostracizing a young girl and her illegitimate baby because the girl refuses (like her obvious ancestor in *The Scarlet Letter*) to name the father of her child. His distorted views lead him to deprive the girl of her livelihood and jeopardize the life of the infant she can no longer support. Phineas' conscience is clear, however, because he regards the innocent baby as the "fruits of the sin."

The incident with Phineas and the girl is prophetic because it foreshadows the family's treatment of Oparre. If this were not sufficient, another parallel to the plight of the Malay princess and her American husband is given on the occasion when Mrs. McQueston and her newly returned son meet. The woman tells Nathaniel a tragic tale:

> There was a man of Salem once who married
> an Indian squaw — and brought her here to live —
> wait till I finish — but they had no neighbors;
> no one spoke to him in the street. He lost
> what work he had. He drank himself to death,
> and the children died. The squaw went back to her tribe,
> and it's said they stoned her. Think well what you
> do before you fetch in this bride. (33)

To placate her now wealthy son (in the interests of the declining family fortune), Mrs. McQueston agrees to receive his family into her home, but her festering resentment is soon noted by the sensitive Oparre, who asks her mother-in-law to reveal what it is that she has done to hurt her. The older woman, unable to contain herself, snaps back: "Your blood! The black blood in your/veins!" (48)

The family opposes the match on two grounds, one of each being demonstrated by the parallel situations discussed above. As the incident with Phineas demonstrates, the Salem devout have a rather muddled notion of what constitutes sin. They

regard Nathaniel's wife as a pagan and they consider the match
a wicked one. Like those students of the Bible who search its
pages for evidence that the races were meant to remain segre-
gated, Phineas and his congregation believe that they are performing a service to society by ignoring the existence of Oparre.
Mrs. McQueston's tale of the ill-fated man of Salem and his
Indian wife introduces the second motive for the family's rejection of Nathaniel's wife. The McQuestons are well aware of
the discriminating practices of the people of the town, as Mrs.
McQueston's tale shows. No doubt the family was among those
who made life difficult for the Indian woman and her husband.
Like all bigots, however, they cannot bear to be discriminated
against themselves. They fear that if Nathaniel and his wife
were to remain permanent members of their household, the
town would shun the entire family. Phineas moans:

> Think of the fingers pointed at me: there's that preacher whose
> brother married a nigger wife and fetched her home! How
> much is a man of God expected to endure? (23)

The setting of Anderson's drama — nineteenth-century
New England — is similar to that of Eugene O'Neill's *Mourning Becomes Electra* in which the destructive effects of distorted Puritanism are responsible for the psychological repres-
sions that plague the Mannons and contribute to their tragedy.
In *The Wingless Victory* that same false view of reality creates
racial prejudices that destroy the marriage of Oparre and her
husband. That prejudice is given an extensive examination by
Anderson. He creates a panoramic vista of the community that
excludes Oparre, although the treatment here varies somewhat
from that of *Asie*. The bigotry confronting Lenormand's heroine is just as intense as it is in Salem; the difference consists of
the way in which it is presented. Except for one incident involving the children at school, we do not see society at large in
the French drama. Rather, all the community disapproval is
concentrated in one figure, De Listrac. What is most interesting
about the prejudice theme, of course, is that it does exist in

both plays. The fact is that its origin is detectable in the myth. Jason and Medea, we recall, lived in Corinth because they received sanctuary there. They were banished from Jason's land, Iolcus, following the violent death of Pelias, the usurper-king, which was contrived by Medea. The expulsion of the couple from Jason's native land is, in essence, a rejection of Medea by Jason's society. It is so interpreted by the French and the American dramatists, who — like all artists — require only a hint to set their creative imaginations working. What is new about the modern plays is that the rejection is based on unreasoned hatred, the heroines being innocent of any crimes in their husbands' homeland.

Only two members of the town's citizenry support Nathaniel. They are his brother, Ruel, whom Phineas has described as a "wastrel" for his less conservative habits, and Faith Ingalls. Faith is the Creusa of the American drama. A somewhat pathetic Creusa, Faith is the girl Nat left behind when he went abroad. She is not a relatively recent acquaintance of the hero's, as was her Greek counterpart. She has known him and loved him for some time, and although she is foolish enough to remain in love with the married Nathaniel, she has — unlike the Corinthian princess of the legend — no hope of marrying him herself. He never encourages her. Volunteering that she has heard from him only once while he was away, she concludes, "He's forgotten me. . . ." (15) Faith is similar to Lenormand's Aimée in that she is portrayed as a particularly understanding and fair person who bears no ill feelings towards the wife of the man she is in love with. She is among the first to greet Oparre, and when tragedy appears imminent, she cautions Nat to leave with his wife. Nevertheless, she is not too good to be true. She confesses that she frequently has thoughts that are somewhat shocking for a well-bred girl. Because of certain prejudices of her own, which she cannot rid herself of completely, and because she loves him, she admits to Nathaniel that she is bothered by the thought of the intimacy that exists between him and his Malay wife:

> I tried not to have the thought — but it haunted me —
> at nights — when you were with her. — It's better, I know
> not to speak of such things. — But we've been friends —
> I wanted to be your friend. And I choke on that —
> it won't go down. (71)

Despite her reservations, the rejected girl proves to be a good friend to the couple. Oparre's fondest wish is that the rest of the town will accept her as Faith does. To that end, the princess expends her energies. However she is, very much like the Medea of the legend, a person with a violent background. This Medea did not murder her brother because she had none, but she may have been responsible for more deaths than was the classical princess. Anderson has his heroine relate that because her father had no son she was his heir. As such, she governed a province and sentenced men to death. She relates the fact that she had been conditioned to the sight of bloodshed since childhood when, on one occasion, her father made her carry a spear with her enemy's head thrust upon it. She continued in this way of life until she met Nathaniel and then, unlike her classical counterpart and unlike Lenormand's heroine, she put aside her violent and strange ways and converted to the somewhat shaky faith of her husband. She narrates the details to her mother-in-law:

> Oh, I had been hard and vengeful too, and taken life in my
> hands! Still somewhere I had heard of a god, the Christ, who
> had pity — and I asked for news of this god. He answered
> mockingly, your son, no lover of gods, till once, at last he gave
> me this little book of the Testaments, and I carry it al-
> ways. (49)

It happens frequently that an individual who marries or forms some close tie with a person not of his social, religious, or ethnic background may be moved to imitate the customs, beliefs, mannerisms, or even speech of that person and the culture from which he springs. The imitation may be conscious or unconscious, sincere or insincere. It has its origin in a desire to approximate the identity of the person being imitated. So Oparre makes an attempt to draw close to Nat by becoming more like his people. Her efforts are conscious and sincere. The religious conversion is one instance. The practice becomes more marked once she is in Salem when she makes an attempt to emulate the New England women she sees passing by her window. She begins by putting aside her Malay chrysalis and assuming Western dress. She takes pleasure in Faith's praise of the gown which she made herself and is encouraged to hope that the women of the town will invite her to their sewing circle. Unfortunately, Oparre's efforts prove in vain. Although she has patiently described to Phineas the transformation she has undergone from barbarian to Christian, Phineas responds by requesting more details of the barbarism she has admitted to. As she looks down upon her beautiful handiwork, she exclaims, "If only this swarthy face/of mine were not above it." (74)

The townspeople are hypocrites, and they continue to snub the pair even though many of the men are in debt to Nathaniel, whose plan it has been to lend money and to make numerous investments in various Salem enterprises. The town rewards him by sending a Bailiff to his door with a summons to appear in court and show cause why he has not given bond for two "slaves." Oparre feels discouraged.

And furthermore, she becomes increasingly aware of the fact that by attempting to approximate the culture of Nat's people she is betraying her own. In connection with this, a minor motif present in *The Wingless Victory,* as in Lenormand's play, is the missionary theme. The criticism is leveled by Anderson against individuals who are well-intentioned in their efforts to support those who bring truth and comfort to their foreign brethren but who err because they lack sufficient sensitivity to foreign customs to understand the character of the people they relate to. Such is the case with the upright citizens of Salem. Oparre speaks of the concern of the good wives of the town for people of lands similar to her own:

> You know they sew
> for foreign missions. They sit in a circle there

> conversing of the scandals of this world —
> mostly of me — while making decent garments
> for little heathen girls across the seas
> that run stark naked. It's a sweet thought; no, truly,
> it is sweet of them. (77)

Oparre has heard that the women have been passing around a picture of ten little native children, all naked, captured in a moment of play on one of their islands, and she has heard that the women detected a resemblance between herself and one of the little natives. Half-desirous of joining that circle and half-conscious that if she does so she will deny her own culture, she tells her husband that she will go to the Salem sewing circle any way that pleases the women:

> Oh any way
> that pleases them, take off my clothes, perhaps,
> and pose there for their little savage child,
> grown older, if it would help. (77–8)

Matters come to a head when the worthies of the town discover a secret about Nathaniel and his past adventure. A diary has been uncovered giving evidence of the fact that Nathaniel's ship "The Queen of the Celebes" is actually the "Nike Apteros," or, translated, "The Wingless Victory," and she is out of The Hague. Delighted with this piece of news, Phineas now has a weapon to use against Nathaniel to force him to be more reasonable about including Oparre as a member of the family, namely an accusation of piracy. An exasperated Nathaniel is finally forced, in his own defense, to tell his brother the details of his past adventure:

> I was a prisoner once to a certain sultan in the Celebes. He was
> Oparre's father, and refused to trade with foreigners, hated the
> Dutch because they'd burned his villages some years before I
> came there. Well, a Dutch ship came in looking for spice, and
> we persuaded him to load it up and then capture it. We
> wanted to get away, Oparre and I. We took three Dutchmen
> who survived and stole the ship from the sultan — ran toward
> Singapore — on the way these three decided to wrest the ship

from me and I shot them down. The rest you know. I managed
to pick up a crew and get home. The ship was forfeit before I
took it. The Dutch had no more claim than I had to it. (91–2)

In viewing Anderson's hero in relation to the hero of *Asie*
and recalling that each descends from the mythological Jason,
it is possible to appreciate the diverse characterization which
the two dramatists achieve. Both begin with the same outline:
Jason is an adventurer, a bold stranger in a foreign land who
uses his wits and his charm to pursue his goal and to extricate
himself from a number of difficulties. He is clever, ambitious,
and handsome. His exploits provide a pattern of action for his
modern counterparts. The contemporary artist, simply by
adding some necessary details, breathes new life into the character and makes him a part of his creation without destroying
its essential unity. Regardless of additions, of course, the
archetypal figure is always visible to the discerning eye. On
the surface De Mezzana appears to have little in common with
Nathaniel McQueston. The surface differences fall away, however, when the artist permits some skeletal structure to show.
For as Anderson's hero tells of the way in which he escaped
imprisonment by his wife's father, we hear an echo of De Mezzana's account of the way in which he and Katha outwitted
and betrayed the ruler of Sibang. The tale of both men are
variations on the original one, that of the flight of Jason and
Medea, who escaped the pursuing Aeetes, king of Colchis, and
hastily retreated to the "Argo." In the Greek tale, the ship
Jason commands is worthy of note because its existence represents the accomplishment of a challenging task. The builder
Argus, working under commission to Jason, performed something of a feat when he constructed a vessel capable of accom-
modating fifty men. The American dramatist, however, makes
his captain an illegitimate one, thus altering a detail of the
ancient story that, until now, has held little thematic interest.
His purpose is to create an immediate cause for the hero's
separation from his wife and to demonstrate the extent of the
prejudice that exists against Nathaniel and Oparre. Phineas
tells his brother that his story will never be believed in an

admiralty court. However, if he sends Oparre back to her people, the evidence against him will be burned. The community uses Nathaniel's questionable ownership of his vessel as an excuse to ostracize the woman and her children condemned as evil by its confused concept of sin.

The minister continues to mouth the belief that the marriage is sinful. Questioning the legality and religious sanction of the marriage ceremony that united the pair, it is an indignant Phineas who causes us to remember that aspect of the myth which dealt with this matter:

> When you put in at New Bedford
> on your way home, you sought out a minister
> and asked him to marry you — but he refused
> What words you may have mumbled over yourself
> and her, on the high seas, I don't know. But she
> is not legally your wife. (93)

Nathaniel is faced with a choice. He can send Oparre away, or he can sail away with her, leaving behind him, to the gain of the gluttonous Salem men, the fortune he has tied up in investments, that same fortune which he risked his life to acquire. The choice is between love or money. We know which one he will choose because Nathaniel is Jason, the ambitious Jason, who wished to marry Creusa because she was the daughter of the king of Corinth, who had promised his future son-in-law a good job. The modern Jason tries to defend his choice to Oparre, reasoning that with "no cash — no home" (104) love would not be enough to sustain them. Oparre is bewildered. Where in the Greek tale the couple find themselves differing on how to live life in the present, Jason arguing for a life of peace and Medea, unable to help herself, inadvertently speaking for a life of emotional instability, here the opposition is between Nathaniel's preference for a life of ease over one of sacrifice and Oparre's need for love, to which she is prepared to relinquish all the money in the world.

In addition to his taste for gold, Nathaniel has another motive for wanting to send his wife away. Jason's desire to settle down with Creusa to the peaceful life is interpreted by Anderson as a desire of Nathaniel's to free himself from his Malay wife because his society's failure to accept the union has bothered him to the extent that he becomes ashamed of her and begins to hate the woman responsible for his isolation. He describes his feelings to Faith:

> Say
> you'd married as I have — for love — and loved him still —
> and had two dark-skinned children — and you lived
> in a few rooms with this same black love of yours —
> and black children, and a black servant — while the town
> Stepped round you carefully — pointing, whispering,
> never to you — always among themselves —
> laughing a little when you come down the street —
> behind their hands — some excellent jest, no doubt,
> at your expense — It's hard to maintain your love —
> you begin to gnaw at this thing you're chained to, even
> hate where you love — curse at it in secret, curse
> yourself and all the world equally. (71–2)

Oparre gets violent for the first time when she realizes that Nathaniel has decided against going with her. True to the actions of the classical heroine, she resolves on murder. Her motive is a new one, however, and it is one that has been logically prepared for in the preceding scenes. Oparre knows that it is her husband's society, as well as Nathaniel, who is casting her out. She feels remorse, moreover, at having deserted the ways of her people in her desire to embrace those of her husband's. She reveals that the fate which her old gods have ordained for the person who deserts his father's house, against his will, to live with an alien is death, and the same death awaits the children of that union. She resolves on killing herself and the children in order to fulfill the requirements of that belief. By such an action she renounces any loyalty she had sworn to the life of Salem, and she returns to her own people:

> God of the children,
> god of the lesser children of the earth,
> the black, the unclean, the vengeful, you are mine

now as when I was a child. He came too soon,
this Christ of peace. Men are not ready yet.
Another hundred thousand years they must drink
your potion of tears and blood. I kneel and adore you,
having blood on my hands, having found it best
that evil be given for evil. Receive me now,
one who might once have been a queen, but followed
after a soft new dynasty of gods
that were not mine. I am punished, and must die. (125–6)

The children must die, too. The youngsters who appear briefly
in this play are little girls rather than boys, the reason becoming
apparent at the end. In addition to the requirements of her
old religion, Oparre kills them so that they will not become
slaves to white men and suffer the accompanying indignities.

At no time is the traditional motive given for the heroine's
action, jealousy of a rival and hatred of the husband who abandons her for another woman, for Nathaniel never considers
marrying Faith. Although Oparre is aware of Faith's love for
her husband she displays no jealous feelings. She demonstrates,
on the contrary, considerable perception and sympathy for the
kind of unhappiness Faith cannot hide. When the girl refuses
her offer of continued friendship and hastily leaves the house
in which Nathaniel and Oparre are living, the older woman is
moved to explain, to her husband, "It's that she loved you/and
it comes to mind." (75) Such a statement is beyond the powers
of the legendary heroine, as it is beyond those of Lenormand's
Katha. Oparre offers Nathaniel no choice such as that held out
to her husband by the heroine of *Asie*. When, at the end of the
drama, her husband changes his mind and comes begging her
forgiveness, she tells him,

You I forgive,
but not your tribe or race — or the white of your hands,
the insult I have had the blood in me
will not forgive. — It will be no man's slave,
nor will my daughters! (129)

The victory Oparre has won over Nathaniel, finally, is a
hollow one because she has already administered the poison to
herself and to her children. Even at this point, when a less

noble woman would attempt to hurt him, Oparre tries to spare him the knowledge that she and their daughters are doomed. After their deaths, Nathaniel, accompanied now by Ruel, sails away from Salem, never to return again. Thus they reject the society that had rejected them.

A formidable challenge advanced by the Medea myth is the call upon the dramatist to evoke some means of bringing the tragedy close to everyday reality. The various modernistic techniques that are employed, such as the anachronisms and the colloquial speech (discernible even in Anderson's verse), serve to dispel the remoteness, the archaic quality of the ancient account. Plot structure is altered; new characters are created; "homey" atmospheric tones are introduced. Most significantly, the canvas is widened. The conflict between the two principal characters is enlarged. Essentially a lovers' quarrel, the counteraction becomes an opposition between two worlds — worlds which we can locate in our own time.

## ✻ NOTES

[1] Mercier-Campiche, op. cit., p. 71.

[2] Jean Giraudoux, La Guerre de Troie n'aura pas lieu (Paris: Bernard Grasset, 1935), pp. 22–23. All subsequent page references to this edition will be given immediately after the quotation.

[3] Laurent Lesage has commented on the fact that the farcical treatment of the Greek characters lends an air of parody to the work. See Lesage, op. cit., pp. 187–88.

[4] See Robert Graves, The Greek Myths (Penguin Books: Baltimore, 1955), Vol. II, pp. 273–74.

[5] The letter is reproduced in Gaetano Salvemini, "Lauro DeBosis," Il Ponte, IV (Gennaio, 1942), pp. 15–6.

[6] The French work was later found to be a translation of a sonnet by the Italian poet Sannazaro.

[7] Lauro DeBosis, Icaro (Milano: Edizioni "Alpes," 1930), p. 21. All subsequent page references to this edition will be given immediately after the quotation.

[8] The leaflet from which this passage is taken, along with the others that the young author dropped on Rome, have been translated and published in Italy To-Day, ed. Mrs. V. M. Crawford, Second Series, Nos. 11 and 12 (Nov.-Dec., 1931), pp. 17–20.

[9] Ibid., p. 19.

[10] H. R. Lenormand, Asie in Théâtre Complet, IX (Paris: Albin Michel, 1938), p. 12. All subsequent page references to this edition will be given immediately after the quotation.

[11] Maxwell Anderson, The Wingless Victory (Washington, D.C.; Anderson House, 1936), p. 32. All subsequent page references to this edition will be given immediately after the quotation.

# ⚜ Conclusion

The return to Greek mythology serves the dramatist in a number of ways. Of major importance is the fact that because the myth enjoys a unique existence outside the flux of time, its aesthetic images are not bound to time and space. Such elasticity allows the modern dramatist to create events and characters that are believable and relevant to contemporary experience. Once the situations around which the ancient tales spin are abstracted, they are found to be of general interest and significance. The Orestes myth, to give one example, reduces itself to the tale of a man who returns home after an absence of a number of years, sets right an old grievance within his house and departs again. Starting with this bare outline, the modern artist begins to add certain elements which result in creating an entirely new view of the hero's experience. The home to which Harry, the Orestes of T. S. Eliot's *The Family Reunion*, returns is an unhappy one because his parents were unable to reconcile their different views of life and could not love one another. Similarly, the setting right of the grievance for the hero of Jean-Paul Sartre's *Les Mouches* involves performing an act that enables him to define the sort of individual he is. It is not possible to overestimate the importance of the central situation in provoking dramatic conflict and giving rise to further action. When it is the myth that provides the situation, it is the myth that is providing the means of ordering and shaping the work itself.

Enjoying considerable freedom in manipulating his material, the artist allows a tale to grow and change to suit the purposes of his creation. Often, the details he adds to complete his interpretation of a tragic history are foreign to the myth. Eugene O'Neill makes of the family to which his Orestes belongs in *Mourning Becomes Electra* a sea-worthy family of Puritans because grievances issue directly from a clash between a distorted Puritan view of life and a romantic outlook. Beneath the surface details, however, the order of the myth is visible, molding and unifying the continuum of stage action. There is no guessing concerning the dramatic future; the story will unfold predictably, inevitably, as it has done for centuries. All the interest is concentrated in the surface details. We are concerned not with what will happen next but how it will happen, for in those details is revealed the dramatist's highly personal view of the oft-told tale. Furthermore many apparently superfluous bits of information take on relevancy when we view the new character or event the playwright has created.

The search into the past has revealed some striking themes which have relevancy for a twentieth-century audience. The question of exile and reconciliation, which in the Orestes tale involves a physical exile and a reconciliation with family and community, is interpreted as the hero's emotional and intellectual experience. Exile for T. S. Eliot equals an alienation from one's God, and reconciliation is viewed as a perception of divine grace and love. The theme of marital discord that emerges from the Medea tale is given a modern social reality by playwrights like H. R. Lenormand and Maxwell Anderson, who view the discord as a result of local prejudices and individual differences based upon the fact that the couple involved represent two different cultures.

Often, to the traditional themes, which are reinterpreted and modernized, playwrights have added new themes that have been suggested by the central situation of the myth and which bring heretofore unexplored meanings to the surface of the old tale. To the ancient theme of vengeance that the characters and the plot of the myth of the House of Atreus serve to advance, Jean Giraudoux has added a completely original motif: the rebellion theme. Electra's clash with Aegisthus is viewed by the contemporary French dramatist as the clash between the princess who seeks absolute justice and the illegitimate ruler who dreams of perfecting the society over which he holds sway and who pleads with the adamant princess for forgiveness and aid in realizing his dream. The originality of Jean Cocteau's *La Machine infernale* is due in large part to the fact that although he has made use of the theme of the quest of Oedipus for the slayer of Laius, Cocteau has portrayed the king of Thebes as a young man in search of his mother. The theme of the neurotic attachment of son to mother predominates. Very often, the theme discernible in the myth serves as an ironic contrast to the new themes the story helps to illustrate. Certainly one of the significant themes of the legend of Orpheus and Eurydice concerns the power and magic of art to create beauty such as that which is capable of illuminating the darkness of the underworld. However the theme of Tennessee Williams' *Orpheus Descending* tells us that the modern Orpheus will never succeed in charming the inhabitants of the lower regions, for although the beauty that the poet creates is eternally the same, his modern audience — preoccupied with the concerns of their daily insignificant lives — have not the capacity or the inclination to understand him, and they turn dull ears to his song.

Most interesting is the portrayal by contemporary artists of previously developed characters with recognized personality traits. Still preserving the original delineation, authors have shaded in various complexities to create new beings to people their plays. The Antigone of the legend who defied Creon because his principles opposed her own remains essentially the same girl in Anouilh's rendering of the story. She, however, has become a purist who scorns compromise, and the principle she speaks for, a principle which shapes her existence, affirms that an individual may defy the political-social order of her state in the interests of preserving laws that are dictated by her conscience. Her belief that the individual alone is the source of ultimate reality is the mark of the modern rebel, the person who protests that because no cosmic order manifests itself, no creating and benevolent God exists to legislate moral conduct, he must turn inward and create his own values. When the portrait is completed, the character may be far removed from the legendary figure on which he is based, as in the case of the character just alluded to, but he owes his existence to his model, for his actions follow the same essential pattern.

Occasionally, a playwright will transform completely a traditional character, but even in such a case, he relies on a known history to develop a new characterization. For example, Egisthe in Giraudoux's *Electre* is a character whose background is the same as that of his classical counterpart. He is a murderer who killed Agamemnon, usurped the throne of Argos, and formed an illicit union with Clytemnestra. His transformation into a benevolent ruler and generally well-intentioned individual is all the more striking because we know he has entertained opposite sentiments. In the case of Richardson's Orestes the dramatist's complete conception depends upon a shock effect accomplished when the audience realizes that the hero the dramatist has created is the opposite in belief and objectives of the mythical character whose name he bears.

In addition to developing and wielding to his own purposes characters already present in the myth, the contemporary playwright also creates completely new figures of his own. The new characters interact with the traditional ones to precipitate the plot along on its preordained route. Jean Giraudoux was particularly inventive in this area. The character Agathe (despite her Greek-sounding family name) is a pure creation of the French author's; her activity marks a sharp departure from the traditional outline of the plot. However, she is the means whereby Electre discovers the truth about Clytemnestre, an event which is crucial to the order of the myth. Similarly, the poet Demokos was never at Troy. Nevertheless, in *La Guerre de Troie n'aura pas lieu* he is instrumental in starting the Trojan War. Phineas in Maxwell Anderson's *The Wingless Victory* is another good example of a character who springs directly from the modern playwright's imagination yet whose activity is essential to the traditional story. In holding out a threat of legal prosecution Phineas provides Nathaniel McQueston, the Jason of the American drama, with a motive for leaving his Medea.

The ancient tales are a particularly fertile source of rich symbolic devices. Often the traditional character will function as a symbol himself. Such is the case with Hélène of *La Guerre de Troie n'aura pas lieu*. She is not only the beautiful woman of legendary fame; she is, to the men of Troy, the very symbol of beauty as she is, further, a symbol of their virility. The two women of Lenormand's *Asie*, Katha and Aimée — who stand for Medea and Creusa — are symbols of the land and the culture to which they are native. The Sphinx of *La Machine infernale* is a particularly interesting figure. Cocteau transforms the mysterious Sphinx of the legend into a charmingly warm-blooded girl at the same time that he has her symbolize a maternal figure, representing the primal trauma.

Frequently, the dramatist will create and impose symbols from outside the tale to clarify the dramatic situation. Such is the case with the powerful symbol of the flies in *Les Mouches*. The bloated flies, which represent the remorse of the Argives, may not be unheard of in Greek mythology, but they are a new addition to the Orestes myth, and they help Sartre illuminate the nature of the error from which his hero rescues the people of Argos. Such is also the case with the snakeskin jacket, which represents the untamed spirit of Tennessee Williams' Orpheus. Snakes, of course, abound in mythology; there is even one in the Orpheus myth itself: Eurydice's death is caused by a snake which bites her as she flees the advancing shepherd. However, unless we stretch the point by suggesting that the reason why Williams' Eurydice is so anxious to see the poet in a navy blue suit is that she fears he will desert her in his "wild" jacket, thus causing her death, one must conclude that the symbol is original. One symbol that is unquestionably foreign to the tale in which it plays an important part is the South Sea island of Orin Mannon's imagination in *Mourning Becomes Electra*. The island represents, for O'Neill's Orestes, a paradise of exclusive maternal love.

Aside from the fact that many artists found similar material for inspiration in the Greek myths, and aside from the fact that their method in reinterpreting those myths followed the same process, the resulting plays are strikingly different from one another, for the men who created them were different. Excluding the imitators, each author views a particular tale in terms of what has greatest meaning for him, in terms of what relates to his frame of reference. Consequently, he will seize on and develop that phase of the myth that allows him to present his own vision. As we have seen, dramatists like Jean Cocteau, Eugene O'Neill, and Tennessee Williams see man as psychologically motivated, reacting under the pressure of impulses he feels compelled to obey. Such is the way, as a result, that O'Neill sees Orestes, Electra, and all the members of Atreus' cursed brood. For people like T. S. Eliot and Jean-Paul Sartre, however, interested in the philosophical and religious implications of Orestes' story, the myth yielded an account of certain ethical and moral conflicts. The Orestes they create represents their personal ethical position.

Some of the dramas discussed above have been set in modern times; others occur in a classical age and even preserve the classical unities. For the most part, regardless of setting, the dramatists have sprinkled in numerous anachronisms to aid the audience in associating its own experience with what is occurring on stage. The dramas, of course, would be just as timely without these additions, but the anachronisms do help in bringing an ancient kingdom close to a nation of the twentieth century, especially when we find evidence of the fact that the sons of Oedipus have been spending long evenings in night clubs. In addition, an attempt has been made to bring the dramas closer to ordinary experience by including more minor figures who represent common humanity and who act accordingly. Where a tragedy of a family is involved, the approach is a domestic one. We see the various members involved expressing familiar sentiments. Brothers and sisters tease one another; nurses express concern for their charges; parents express fears for their children. Tragedy is often violent, but frequently the unhappy people involved are more like many people whom we may know. They simply lead lives of quiet desperation.

In many cases an author's personal involvement in the drama and in the myth he recreates — an involvement which, whatever its artistic drawbacks, helps to abbreviate the distance between audience and myth — is apparent from a knowledge of certain biographical details. One knows, for example, that in Tennessee Williams' conception of Tartarus boxes of shoes and shoe-fitting chairs are inevitable; the playwright has revealed that in the summer of 1939 he worked in the Los Angeles area in Clark's Bootery. Within sight were the Elysian Fields — an M.G.M. studio.[1] Similarly, Eugene O'Neill may make of an ancient Greek queen a striking figure with sea-blue eyes and bronze hair and explain the additions by attributing his Clytemnestra with an exotic French-Dutch background, but we know that he is really describing his good-looking Irish mother.

In returning to mythology dramatists were stimulated, ultimately, by a desire to present a broader view of man. What contemporary authors had inherited from their recent cultural past, specifically the last quarter of the nineteenth century, was a view of drama as an occasion for the representation of individual man. Naturalistic doctrines declared that man was decipherable as the product of a number of impersonal forces (defined mainly by Darwin, Marx, and Freud). Their attention given over to a scientific study of human behavior, writers began to create modern social and psychological drama. Their aim was to approximate reality. However in drawing "round" characters they frequently created psychological case studies, and while attempting to reveal that people do indeed do the sort of things that their characters do, they presented the uncommon individual and the uncommon situation.

The value of the mythological character rests precisely in the fact that he is not an individual but a type, an archetype, in fact. Larger than life, he embodies a universal truth. Each member of the audience, regardless of social milieu or psychological drives, can see part of himself in the archetypal character. Where the individual is a reduction, a particular segment of humanity, the archetype is an enlargement, encompassing all men. One may not be willful like Antigone, but one experiences moments of willfulness — whether or not one was spoiled as a child. Thus, in her willfulness, Antigone incarnates those streaks of stubbornness we may detect in ourselves. Furthermore, because all intimate details concerning the archetypal hero — his personality traits, background, and so on are not known to us, he retains an enigmatic quality. He can be constantly redefined, reshaped in the image of the writer who revitalizes him and who believes, finally, that he has solved the mystery surrounding the character, even if he does so only to his own satisfaction. That aspect of the character that is known provides the base on which the dramatist builds his own hero, simply by filling in the missing details. If it so happens that the dramatist insists upon seeing the mythological hero as psychologically motivated, it is to his advantage that the character be an abstraction. He can proceed to develop his own theories (at most only partially scientific) without having to dispute any existing ones. The playwright is free to define the character from any point of view he chooses.

It is in this sense — by providing archetypal characters that can be redefined in ever-changing forms — that the myth makes art possible, as T. S. Eliot maintains. One recalls, too, the statement of Jean-Paul Sartre's that the myth integrates life, presents man in his entirety, which is another way of saying that the archetype leads the dramatist away from a limited view of man.

By going to ancient tragedies and transforming, reinterpreting, and reviving them to suit the vision of a twentieth-century audience, the various artists are involved in a search, a search for most effective ways of communicating the truths they would express. Drama is where they find it. The situations and the figures they handle may appear to be remote from everyday life, but they are not. The resulting plays are often shocking in their manner of handling the classical material. However in combining the permanent mythical image with modern means of interpretation, the playwright — if he is successful at his craft — achieves a work that possesses its own lasting beauty, and he reaffirms the oneness of our culture.

Speaking of other plays and other playwrights, Eric Bentley sums up our thoughts: "When a new play is, at the same time, shockingly old-fashioned and outrageously new-fangled, one should perhaps begin to wonder if it is not a classic."[2]

## ✳ NOTES

[1] Tennessee Williams, "The Past, The Present and The Perhaps," in *Orpheus Descending: Battle of Angels, op. cit.*, p. viii.

[2] Eric Bentley, "Afterword" in *The Classic Theatre*, Vol. IV: *Six French Plays* (New York: Doubleday & Co. Inc., 1961), p. xv.

# ※ Bibliography

Albérès, René-Marill. *Esthétique et morale chez Giraudoux.* Paris: Nizet, 1962.

Alexander, Doris M. "Psychological Fate in *Mourning Becomes Electra*," *PMLA*, LXVIII (Dec., 1953), 923–34.

Anderson, Maxwell. *The Wingless Victory.* Washington, D.C.: Anderson House, 1936.

Anouilh, Jean. *Antigone* in *Nouvelles pièces noires.* Paris: Table Ronde, 1958.

Arrowsmith, William. "The Criticism of Greek Tragedy," *The Tulane Drama Review*, III (March, 1959), 41–5.

Asselineau, Roger. "*Mourning Becomes Electra* as a Tragedy," *Modern Drama*, I (Dec., 1958), 143–50.

Barber, C. L. "Strange Gods at T. S. Eliot's *The Family Reunion*," in *T. S. Eliot: A Selected Critique*, ed. Leonard Unger. New York: Holt, Reinhart & Winston, Inc., 1948, 415–43.

Barnes, Hazel E. *The Literature of Possibility.* Lincoln: University of Nebraska Press, 1959.

Battenhouse, Roy. "*The Family Reunion* as Christian Prophecy," *Christendom*, X (Sumner, 1945), 307–21.

Bentley, Eric. "Afterword" in *The Classic Theater,* IV, New York: Doubleday & Co., Inc., 1961.

———. *The Life of the Drama.* New York: Atheneum Publishers, 1964.

Bodkin, Maud. *The Quest for Salvation in an Ancient and a Modern Play.* London: Oxford University Press, 1941.

Boorsch, Jean. "The Use of Myths in Cocteau's Theater," *Yale French Studies,* No. 5 (1950), 76–82.

Bowra, C. M. *Sophoclean Tragedy.* Oxford: Oxford University Press, 1944.

Camus, Albert. *L'Homme révolté* in *Oeuvres Complètes.* Paris: Gallimard, 1962.

Cargill, Oscar. *Intellectual America.* New York: The Macmillan Co., 1941.

Carne-Ross, Donald. "The Position of *The Family Reunion* in the Work of T. S. Eliot," *Revista de Letterature Moderne,* Anno I, No. 2, Nuova Serie (Oct., 1950), 125–39.

Champigny, Robert. *Stages on Sartre's Way.* Bloomington: Indiana University Press, 1959.

———. "Theatre in a Mirror," *Yale French Studies,* No. 14 (1954–55), 57–64.

Chase, Robert. *Quest for Myth.* Baton Rouge: Louisiana State University Press, 1949.

Cocteau, Jean. *La Machine infernale.* Paris: Bernard Grasset, 1934.

Conacher, D. J. "Orestes as Existentialist Hero," *Philological Quarterly,* 33 (Oct., 1954), 404–10.

———. "Some Euripidean Techniques in the Dramatic Treatment of Myth," *University of Toronto Quarterly,* XXII (1952–3), 55–71.

Cranston, Maurice. *Sartre.* London: Oliver & Boyd Ltd., 1962.

Diez Del Corral, Luis. *La Función del mito clásico en la literatura contemporanea.* Madrid: Editorial Grados, 1957.

De Bosis, Lauro. *Icaro.* Milano: Edizioni "Alpes," 1930.

Eliot, T. S. *The Family Reunion.* New York: Harcourt, Brace & World, Inc., 1950.

————. *The Family Reunion* in *Playwrights on Playwriting*, ed. Toby Cole. New York: Hill & Wang, Inc., 1960, 254–57.

————. *Four Quartets*. New York: Harcourt, Brace & World, Inc., 1943.

————. *Selected Essays*. New York: Harcourt, Brace & World, Inc., 1950.

————. *"Ulysses,* Order, & Myth" in *Forms of Modern Fiction*, ed. William Van O'Connor. Minneapolis: University of Minnesota Press, 1948, 120–24.

————. "Virgil and the Christian World," *Sewanee Review*, LXI (1953), 1–14.

Engel, Edwin A. *The Haunted Heroes of Eugene O'Neill*. Cambridge: Harvard University Press, 1953.

Falk, Doris. *Eugene O'Neill and the Tragic Tension*. New Brunswick: Rutgers University Press, 1958.

Falk, Signi L. *Tennessee Williams*. New York: Twayne Publishers, Inc., 1961.

Fergusson, Francis. *The Idea of a Theater*. Princeton: Princeton University Press, 1949.

————. "Sartre as Playwright," *Partisan Review*, XVI (April, 1949), 407–11.

Gardner, Helen. *The Art of T. S. Eliot*. New York: E. P. Dutton & Co., Inc., 1950.

Gassner, John. "At War With *Electre,*" *The Tulane Drama Review*, III, No. 4 (May, 1959), 42–50.

————. *Theatre At The Crossroads*. New York: Holt, Rinehart, & Winston, Inc., 1960.

Giraudoux, Jean. *Electra* in *Théâtre*. V. III, Paris: Bernard Grasset, 1959.

————. *La Guerre de Troie n'aura pas lieu*. Paris: Bernard Grasset, 1935.

Goheen, Robert F. *The Imagery of Sophocles' Antigone*. Princeton: Princeton University Press, 1951.

Graves, Robert. *The Greek Myths*. Baltimore: Penguin Books, 1955.

Guicharnaud, Jacques. *Modern French Theatre*. New Haven: Yale University Press, 1961.

Harding, D. W. "Progression of Theme in Eliot's Modern Plays," *The Kenyon Review*, XVIII, No. 3 (Summer, 1956), 337–60.

Hatzfeld, Helmut. *Trends and Styles in Twentieth Century French Literature.* Washington, D.C.: The Catholic University of America Press, 1957.

Highet, Gilbert. *The Classical Tradition: Greek and Roman Influences on Western Literature.* New York: Oxford University Press, 1949.

Inskip, Donald. *Jean Giraudoux, The Making of a Dramatist.* London: Oxford University Press, 1958.

*Italy To-Day.* ed. Mrs. V. M. Crawford. Second Series, Nos. 11 & 12 (Nov.–Dec., 1931).

Jeanson, Francis. *Sartre par lui-même.* Paris: Aux Editions du Seuil, 1955.

Jones, David E. *The Plays of T. S. Eliot.* London: Routledge & Kegan Paul, 1961.

Jones, Frank. "Scenes from the Life of Antigone," *Yale French Studies,* No. 6 (1950), 91–100.

Joyce, James. *A Portrait of the Artist as a Young Man.* New York: The Viking Press, 1963.

Kanters, Robert. *"L'Usage des mythes,"* *Cahiers du Sud,* XIX, No. 219 (Aug.–Sept., 1939), 51–6.

Kitto, H. D. F. *Greek Tragedy: A Literary Study.* New York: Doubleday & Co., Inc., 1954.

Langer, Susanne K. *Feeling and Form.* New York: Charles Scribner's Sons, 1953.

Lenormand, H. R. *Asie in Théâtre Complet.* IX, Paris: Albin Michel, 1938.

Lesage, Laurent. *Jean Giraudoux, His Life and His Works.* University Park: Pennsylvania State University Press, 1959.

Libel, Maurice. *"Actualité d'Eschyle,"* *La Revue de L'Université Laval,* XII (1952), 105–19.

Matthiessen, F. O. *The Achievement of T. S. Eliot.* London: Oxford University Press, 1947.

Mercier-Campiche, Marianne. *Le Théâtre de Giraudoux et la condition humaine.* Paris: Domat, 1954.

Mohrt, Michel. *Montherlant "Homme Libre"* Paris: Gallimard, 1943.

Montherlant, Henry de. *Pasiphaé* in *Théâtre de Montherlant*. Paris: Gallimard, 1954.

Mullahy, Patrick. *Oedipus, myth and complex*. New York: Hermitage Press, 1948.

O'Neill, Eugene. *Mourning Becomes Electra* in *Nine Plays*. New York: Random House, Inc., 1954.

————. "Working Notes and Extracts from a Fragmentary Work Diary," in *European Theories of the Drama*, ed. Barrett H. Clark. New York: Crown Publishers, Inc., 1947, 534–36.

Oxenhandler, Neal. *Scandal & Parade: The Theater of Jean Cocteau*. New Brunswick: Rutgers University Press, 1957.

Peter, John. "The Family Reunion," *Scrutiny*, XVI (1949), 219–30.

Popkin, Henry. "The Plays of Tennessee Williams," *The Tulane Drama Review*, IV (Spring, 1960), 57–66.

Poujol, Jacques. *"Tendresse et cruauté dans le théâtre de Jean Anouilh,"* French Review, XXV, No. 5 (April, 1952), 337–47.

Poulet, Georges. *Studies in Human Time*, tr. Elliott Coleman. Baltimore: The Johns Hopkins Press, 1956.

Pratt, Norman T. "Aeschylus and O'Neill: Two Worlds," *Classical Journal*, 51 (Jan. 1956), 163–7.

Pronko, Leonard Cabell. *The World of Jean Anouilh*. Berkeley and Los Angeles: University of California Press, 1961.

Pucciani, Oreste F. *The French Theater Since 1930*. Boston: Ginn and Co., 1954.

Rahv, Philip. "The Myth and the Powerhouse," *Partisan Review*, XX (Nov.–Dec., 1953), 635–47.

Rank, Otto. *The Trauma of Birth*. New York: Robert Brunner, 1952.

Richardson, Jack. *The Prodigal*. New York: E. P. Dutton & Co., Inc., 1960.

Russell, Claire and W. M. S. *Human Behavior*. Boston: Little, Brown & Co., 1961.

Salvemini, Gaetano. "Lauro De Bosis," *Il Ponte*, IV (Jan., 1942), 9–31.

200 ❊ ANCIENT GREEK MYTHS AND MODERN DRAMA

Sartre, Jean-Paul. *L'Existentialisme est un humanisme.* Paris: Nagel, 1946.

——. "Forgers of Myth: the Young Playwrights of France," *Theatre Arts,* XXX (June, 1946), 324–35.

——. *Huis Clos; Les Mouches.* Paris: Gallimard, 1947.

Scott, Nathan A., Jr. *Rehearsals of Discomposure.* New York: Columbia University Press, 1952.

Skinner, Richard Dana. *Eugene O'Neill: A Poet's Quest.* New York: Longmans, Green & Co., 1935.

Slochower, Harry. "The Function of Myth in Existentialism," *Yale French Studies,* I, No. 1, 42–52.

Smidt, Kristian. *Poetry and Belief in the Work of T. S. Eliot.* London: Routledge & Kegan Paul, 1961.

Smith, Carol H. *T. S. Eliot's Dramatic Theory and Practice.* Princeton: Princeton University Press, 1963.

Smith, Grover Jr. *T. S. Eliot's Poetry and Plays.* Chicago: University of Chicago Press, 1956.

Smith, Winifred. "Greek Heroines in Modern Dress," *Sewanee Review* (July–Sept., 1941), 385–96.

Sørensen, Hans. *Le Théâtre de Jean Giraudoux* in *Acta Jutlandica.* Aersskrift for Aarhus Universitet #22, Supplementary Humanistic Series #35, Copenhagen: Ejnar Munksgaard, 1950.

Spoerri, Theophil. "The Structure of Existence: *The Flies,*" in *Sartre: A Collection of Critical Essays,* ed. Edith Kern, Englewood Cliffs: Prentice-Hall, Inc., 1962, 54–61.

Steiner, George. *The Death of Tragedy.* New York: Alfred A. Knopf, Inc., 1961.

Tischler, Nancy M. *Tennessee Williams: Rebellious Puritan.* New York: The Citadel Press, 1961.

Trilling, Lionel. "The Genius of O'Neill," in *O'Neill and His Plays,* ed. Oscar Cargill, N. Bryllion Fagin, and William J. Fisher. New York: New York University Press, 1961, 296–302.

Unger, Leonard. *The Man in the Name: Essays on the Experience of Poetry.* Minneapolis: The University of Minnesota Press, 1956.

Ward, Anne. "Speculations on Eliot's Time-World: An Analysis of *The Family Reunion* in relation to Hulme and Bergson," *American Literature*, XXI ( 1949), 18–34.

Watts, Richard, Jr. "Orpheus Descending," *Theatre Arts*, XLII (Sept., 1958), 24–28.

Weales, Gerald. *American Drama Since World War II*. New York: Harcourt, Brace & World, Inc., 1962.

Wheelwright, Philip. *Heraclitus*. Princeton: Princeton University Press, 1959.

Williams, Tennessee. *Orpheus Descending: Battle of Angels*. New York: James Laughlin, 1958.

————. "The Past, The Present and The Perhaps" in *Orpheus Descending: Battle of Angels*. New York: James Laughlin, 1958.

Winther, Sophus Keith. *Eugene O'Neill: A Critical Study*. New York: Russell and Russell, 1961.

Young, Stark. *Immortal Shadows*. New York: Charles Scribner's Sons, 1948.